La Bella Vita

Daily Inspiration from Italy

Helen Ruchti

XYZZY PRESS

Copyright 2008 © Xyzzy Press

For information about permission to reproduce selections from this book, write to Permissions, Xyzzy Press, 9105 Concord Hunt Circle, Brentwood, TN 37027

 Library of Congress Cataloging-in-Publication Data

Ruchti, Helen.
 La bella vita : daily inspiration from Italy / by Helen Ruchti.
   p. cm.
 ISBN-13: 978-1-60148-012-5 (softcover)
 ISBN-10: 1-60148-012-1 (softcover)
 1. Devotional calendars--Baptists. 2. Ruchti, Helen--Travel--Italy. 3. Italy--Description and travel. I. Title.
 BV4811.R73 2008
 242'.2--dc22

                              2007050363

Jacket and Interior design by Birdsong Creative, Franklin, Tennessee
www.birdsongcreative.com

Printed in the United States of America
10 9 8 7 6 5 4 3 2 1

Dedication

To the "Saints in Rome"—Rome, Italy, and Rome, Georgia—with whom

my husband, William C. Ruchti, Jr., and I worked throughout our ministry.

With grateful appreciation for the amazing love, generosity, partnership

in the Gospel, and prayerful support of faithful members of Rome Baptist

Church (English language) in Italy, and of Fifth Avenue Baptist Church and

First Baptist Church in Rome, Georgia, and for the individual and collective

worldwide witness of our brothers and sisters in Christ.

Table of Contents

III: *Artistic Italy*

IV: *Faithful Italy*

V: *Buon Viaggio!*

Introduction

During the summer of 1959, a Rome, Georgia, department store offered a contest to its regular customers. The prize was two deluxe trips from Rome, Georgia, to Rome, Italy. I entered the winning four-line poem. My husband, William C. Ruchti, Jr.—known also as Dub—and I enjoyed the trip to four European cities. As a result of the journey, our family's life took a new direction.

We both felt called to Rome and, within a year of our first trip, the International Mission Board of the Southern Baptist Convention appointed us to work with English-speaking people in Rome, Italy, where Baptists working at the American Embassy had requested such a ministry.

We arrived in Italy in the fall of 1960 for a year of language study in Perugia. The following year we moved to Rome. Designated for our use was a Baptist chapel that closed during World War II when men were at war and many women and children lived with relatives in the country. The meeting place was in the centuries-old Baptist Union building under renovation. An elevator was being installed, so it was necessary to wait for months for work to be completed and the worship area to be cleared of building materials. On a Friday evening in late summer we had a picnic and prayer meeting on the Appian Way with two American Embassy secretaries, prospects for our future church. When we returned home, Dr. Roy Starmer of the Baptist Publishing House called to say that the worship area in the building at Piazza in Lucina was cleared and we could begin our ministry in the chapel, which had been approved by the government as a place for non-Catholics to worship. The following day we cleaned the worship room and telephoned people we knew who wanted to attend an English-language church. On Sunday, August 15, 1962, on the biggest summer holiday in Italy, 12 Americans gathered for worship in what would later be named Rome Baptist Church (English language).

Our 25 years in Italy seemed to fly by. The Second Vatican Council, the beginnings of the European Union, and a stronger Italian economy brought significant changes to the life of Italians. The days and years were crammed full of interesting activities and encounters with fascinating people from all over the world. Our constantly changing congregation continued to grow. During our last year, about 125 people from 30 nations made up the fellowship of the church. In August 1985, we left Rome, Italy, for our retirement home in Rome, Georgia.

During two and a half decades, we enjoyed the wonder and challenge of living in Italy. We knew hundreds of foreigners who lived temporarily or permanently in Rome. We all shared the quest of understanding the country and its energetic people while enjoying life in Italy. Most any foreigner who lives there immediately becomes a tour guide when his friends pass through or come for a visit. These expatriates buy guidebooks and history books, take tours, ask their Italian friends to explain customs, and learn the language.

This book is the antipasto, the first course of an Italian banquet of people, places, art, music, customs, faith, and determination. It is hoped that the reader will add to his store of knowledge from the facts, observations, secrets, and soul of a nation revealed here. May this book encourage you to travel to Italy or return for another visit. Have a good trip! *Buon viaggio!*

Section I
Beautiful Italy

The Beautiful Life

"He has made everything beautiful in its time."
Ecclesiastes 3:11a

Italy is a popular travel destination because of its pleasant climate, fascinating cities, beautiful countryside, welcoming people, and delicious food. A longtime Rome resident said, "Italy is not just the country you want to see. It's the country you want to go back to again and again." Every Italian city is distinct from others. Traveling from Rome to Venice or from Milan to Naples is almost like being in another country, except for the language. Foreigners who have the good fortune of having a work assignment or long holiday in Italy discover the markets and the abundant supply of fresh fruits and vegetables. To eat well was the reason Elizabeth Gilbert went to Italy for the first part of the journey she recorded in *Eat, Pray, and Love.* In recent years, dining in fine restaurants has become very expensive, but frugal travelers find good fare in popular eateries: *la tavola calda, la trattoria, la rosticceria,* and *il mercato.* In towns and cities the piazza is the neighborhood gathering place and where public functions are held. Walking around the city, standing in the piazza, one enjoys being a part of the community.

The Italians' innate sense of beauty and balance enhances life in their cities. In the country it seems every farmer has built his tidy farmhouse and planted trees in harmony with the landscape. The influence of the Church and of her teachings is felt in the life of the people. The host of people willing to help the overwhelming numbers of foreigners who tour or live among them far outnumber the scoundrels who cheat and steal from unsuspecting travelers.

La bella vita—"the beautiful life"—is relished in Italy by those who love people, art, music, history, food, religious ceremony, plain goodness, the sea, mountains, lakes, farms, towns, cities, archeological sites, travel, and drama in everyday life.

Father, thank you for Italy and for her resilient people.
May they love and serve you.

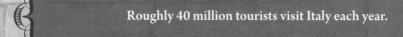

Roughly 40 million tourists visit Italy each year.

Language Learning

"The heavens declare the glory of God; And the firmament shows His handiwork. Day unto day utters speech, And night unto night reveals knowledge. There is no speech nor language where their voice is not heard."

Psalm 19:1-3

Communicating with family and neighbors in your native tongue is as easy as opening your mouth and speaking. You hardly think about it. When we arrived in Italy, it was necessary to study Italian at the University for Foreigners in Perugia. Students from all over the world studied in a cold, drafty baroque palace. Most students from English-speaking countries had a difficult time learning the Latin-based language. Students from France, Spain, Portugal, and Romania easily picked up Italian, as their languages were also corrupt Latin. Students from Germany and Scandinavia easily learned a fourth or fifth language. Students from Asia and Africa had different grammar bases and special learning problems. As a student body, we were separated by language, but we were drawn together by our mutual need to learn to communicate in Italian.

Many Italian friends helped us with conversational Italian. In Perugia, Anna Maria corrected my homework and explained grammar. In Rome, at the newsstand every morning, Anna encouraged Dub to tell her American jokes in Italian, correcting grammar and pronunciation. Edda corrected his sermons, written in Italian, and talked theology with him in English and Italian. We learned to speak with Italians and to translate for foreigners who spoke no Italian. In our early years, Dub sang his order to the butcher who sang back to him in return, entertaining the customers and delighting everyone with their two-bit opera. When asked, "How long did it take you to learn Italian?" I confess, "It takes a lifetime. I'm still learning."

Lord, thank you for the miracle of speech that greatly enhances our life experience.

Italian is the 27th most spoken language in the world and is affectionately called *la lingua melodiosa* by its speakers.

Spaghetti

"…if indeed you have tasted that the Lord is gracious."
I Peter 2:3

"All that I am or hope to be, I owe to spaghetti," said Sophia Loren. Italians like their pasta *al dente*, which literally means "to the teeth," so that the pasta is neither mushy nor crunchy. Most importantly, it is served hot with a memorable sauce. Without pasta, an Italian meal is incomplete. Pasta, brought from Italy to America by immigrants who had their recipes with them, is the first course of a meal. Following the pasta course are meat, vegetables, salad, and then the fruit and cheese.

To eat spaghetti properly, the cautious Italian tucks a cloth napkin into his collar, sprinkles the food with a liberal serving of parmesan cheese, mixes the steaming spaghetti with sauce and cheese, and begins to twirl the spaghetti around his fork. But before taking a bite, he usually acknowledges the marvel of the Italian meal he is ready to enjoy by saluting his table companions with the encouraging words, *"Buon appetito!"*

Some people twirl the fork full of spaghetti with the aid of a tablespoon, but usually a diner merely lifts a few pieces of spaghetti on the fork tines and twirls them against the bottom of the bowl. Sauce remaining in the bottom of the bowl is deftly soaked up by a piece of bread speared by a fork and eaten with gusto. This is an accepted custom that maximizes every tasty bite.

Once in a Bible study, Antonio, a young Italian, commented on the joy of salvation. He said, "If someone told you that spaghettis are good, you wouldn't know what he meant if you had never eaten spaghettis. But once you have tasted them, then you know spaghettis are wonderful." His inconsistent grammar made his testimony all the more charming. Hurray for spaghettis!

Father, give us this day our daily portion of life-sustaining food,
and help us to be grateful for your generosity to us.

Spaghetti literally means "little strings."

Sports

"… let us lay aside every weight, and the sin which so easily ensnares us, and let us run with endurance the race that is set before us."
Hebrews 12:1b

Italy had defeated France to win the World Cup in Berlin! On the night of July 9, 2006, millions of sports fans shouted and cheered in homes and at neighborhood bars. Ecstatic shouts, sounds of piercing automobile horns, and exploding firecrackers filled the air. Coach Marcello Lippi said, "I've won many championships, but a joy so big I have never felt." Not since 1982 when Italy defeated Brazil, the world's top soccer team, had so much patriotic emotion been displayed. Young people drove around all night, honked horns, and shouted *Viva Italia!* In 1982 political analysts commented that the winning of the World Cup did more for national unity than any political movement in recent times. The end of the two World Wars couldn't have been celebrated more joyously.

No doubt about it, Italians love their sports. Best of all, they like *calcio*, which Americans know as soccer and Europeans call football. Raucous sports fans are called *tifosi* or "fever boys." Everyone seems to know the names of celebrity players, and children collect cards of their favorite athletes.

Besides soccer, Italians enjoy basketball, tennis, boating, skiing, bobsledding, racing (of bicycles, motorcycles, cars, horses, and boats) and, a select few, golf. Basketball teams often include tall American players. International tennis championships are held in spring and summer in various cities. Bicycling features *Giro d'Italia*, a cross-country, 25-day bike race in May. Car and motorcycle racing is in Monza in September. An International Horse Show in Rome's Villa Borghese Park attracts the rich and the famous. A sailing regatta is enjoyed at Portofino in September. An international motorboat race, *Del Lario*, takes place on Lake Como in October. Winter sports events are scheduled in the Italian Alps during those months.

Help us, Lord, to keep our bodies in good condition so we can do the work to which you call us.

The 1960 Summer Olympics held in Rome required the city to build adequate arenas. The city of Turin hosted the 2006 Winter Olympics.

Mineral Water

"But the water that I shall give him will become in him a fountain of water springing up into everlasting life."
John 4:14b

In Italy many people drink bottled mineral water—*acqua minerale*—for they prefer the taste or think it is safer than tap water. Mineral water can be plain or sparkling with added carbonation. Some Italians order cases of mineral water and store them in the basement of their villa or on the balcony of their apartment. Rome's restaurants offer a variety of mineral water, a good source of income for them. The customer needs to be sure the bottle is opened in his presence, or else he may pay bottled-water prices for tap water. A waiter often pretends to misunderstand when a diner orders *acqua semplice* or "simple water." Sometimes further explanation convinces the waiter the customer wants *acqua dal rubinetto* or "water from the spigot."

One January day I returned home with several ladies from a prayer retreat at Lake Bracciano, north of the city. We stopped by the springs of Acqua Claudia, near the Via Anguillarese. We drove down a winding road, crossed train tracks, passed by farms and a bottling plant. We finally arrived at the masonry shed where the public has access to the artesian well. People can have all the water they can carry away. Fourteen spigots are constantly spewing out warm, sparkling mineral water. I had brought several jugs and proceeded to fill my bottles.

Funke, a Nigerian, rushed to the flowing water. Her brown eyes sparkled as she realized the wonder of all that free, gushing water. "We don't have anything like this in Nigeria!" she said. "We have wells. But none that flow and flow and flow!" Her enthusiasm for the abundant water was as free-flowing as the well. "Praise the Lord! He is so generous with His riches!" All the way into Rome, Funke praised the Creator for His generosity.

Loving God, thank you for life-sustaining water and for the water of everlasting life that restores our souls.

Mineral wells near Rome provide water for several brand names of bottled water: Acqua Appia, Acqua Sacra, Acqua Olimpia, Acqua San Pietro, Acqua Laurentina, and Acqua Claudia.

Markets

"Oh, taste and see that the Lord is good."
Psalm 34:8a

Shopping at *la fruttavendola*, the neighborhood fruit seller, was a time-saver, but I always felt I had missed something if I didn't go the few extra blocks to the *mercato*. The market closest to our apartment was at Ponte Milvio. Dozens of stalls were arranged under cottonwood trees on a large sidewalk near the 2,000-year-old bridge where Constantine defeated Maxentius in 312. Modern Italians shop much in the manner that their ancestors did. They take their own baskets, buy quantities of food for one meal or enough for the day, and haggle over prices. They enjoy the drama and abundance of the market.

Fruit and vegetable stalls are placed in the same area. Poultry carts are near each other. The smelly fishmongers choose a place near the street and away from the other merchants. Cheese and sandwich-meat stalls offer butter, sardines, tuna fish, and olives. Often a vendor offers only a variety of olives and pickled vegetables. Usually an elderly woman has fresh herbs for sale; she may also sell eggs, which she picks up three at a time and wraps in newspaper.

Merchants work hard, arriving early to set up their stalls. When I asked one vendor what time she got up in the mornings, she said, *"Con i pulcini"* or "with the chickens," which is 2:30!

One spring day, I passed a stall in the market where large red strawberries were lavishly displayed. They looked delicious. The merchant wanted everyone to know he had the best in the market. He called out, *"Fragole belle! Fragole buone! Assaggiate e vedete! Sono buone!"* ("Beautiful strawberries! Sweet strawberries! Taste and see! They are good!") Somewhere in a market in the land of Israel the Psalmist had probably heard a merchant cry, "Taste and see!" and spiritualized the statement. He knew that God is good.

Thank you, Lord, for the abundance of good foods to nourish our bodies.
We have tasted your goodness, and we know it satisfies.

**It is custom to not touch the fruit or vegetables in Italian markets.
Instead gain permission from the vendor before choosing produce.**

Howdy!

"Greet all the brethren with a holy kiss."
I Thessalonians 5:26

A tall tourist, wearing a 10-gallon hat and cowboy boots walked into a Rome neighborhood coffee bar and greeted everyone, "Howdy, folks!" Italians do not normally greet everyone in a room, Texas style. If they don't know you—in other words, haven't been properly introduced, even though you may have lived in the same building for five years— they might not speak to or even look at you. Trying to understand the etiquette sometimes puzzles newcomers.

Buon giorno! or "Good day!" is the standard greeting; adding "sir" or "madam" makes it a little more friendly: *Buon giorno, signore! Buon giorno, signora! Buona sera, signore!* means "Good evening, sir." If the evening is late and you won't see each other again, the final good-bye is *Buona notte! Arrivederci* is another polite way to say "Good-bye." By now the entire world knows the informal greeting and farewell, *Ciao!* It is the salutation of choice of children and good friends.

A firm handshake while looking the person in the eye is the physical part of the greeting or farewell. In their churches, Italian Christians greet each other warmly with a handshake and a holy kiss at the same time. They not only shake hands and greet each other upon arrival, but they shake hands and have a quick kiss on left and right cheeks before leaving a meeting. Shaking hands when greeting anyone is important. If hands are full or dirty, it is customary to rub elbows. Body contact is necessary—a kiss, a handshake, or rubbing elbows. Younger Americans who have traveled abroad or are mimicking celebrities now embrace and kiss when meeting in public. But my generation's proper grandparents never did more than shake hands or nod and smile.

Father, this day may we be pleasant in our contacts with others.

Ciao is derived from the Latin word *schiavo*,
meaning "I am your slave."

One-Way Streets

"Teach me Your way, O LORD, And lead me in a smooth path, because of my enemies."
Psalm 27:11

While we lived there, a cartoon by Helen Burggraff in Rome's *International Daily News* amused expatriates residing there. A camera-carrying, sandal-shod tourist says confidently to his wife, "Don't worry. We won't get lost! I know our hotel's street. It's on *Senso Unico!*" Those two words mean literally "unique direction" or "one-way street." Italy's many one-way streets twist and turn and frustrate inexperienced drivers.

One summer afternoon a tourist called to ask if we could take him sightseeing. "Where are you staying?" I asked. He ran to the window and read the street sign below. "My hotel is on *Senso Unico* Street," he said. "What is the name of your hotel?" I countered, after explaining the street name. "I'll look. It's *Albergo Hotel*. It's on the busy street with the beautiful fountain." The tourist thought I had the necessary information to find him, but as *albergo* means "hotel" in Italian, I only knew that he was in the Hotel Hotel on One-Way Street, a busy avenue near a fountain. Dozens of hotels match that description.

One-way streets have become very common in Italy's crowded cities. When driving, sometimes it is quite complicated to arrive at a specific destination because of the one-way streets and other streets closed to traffic. Before the proliferation of automobiles, nearly every downtown street was open to traffic and was two-way. As traffic increased in the 1970s and 80s, more and more streets became one-way. During one summer Rome's city officials decided to reverse the traffic flow of the one-way streets along the Tiber River, confusing even the Italian drivers. In many Italian cities now, traffic is so congested that downtown areas are completely closed to traffic. Fortunately the many buses, taxis, and sidewalks will take you where you want to go.

Father, help us to be aware, flexible, imaginative, and responsible in our life experiences.

In Italy when someone travels by "the horses of St. Francis," it means his legs will take him.

A Fistful of Parsley

*"And the earth brought forth grass, the herb that yields seed according to its kind,
and the tree that yields fruit, whose seed is in itself according to its kind.
And God saw that it was good."*

Genesis 1:12

"Would you like some *odori?*" is a frequent question at fruit and vegetable markets. A positive response produces immediate action. The green grocer bends down and picks up a handful of parsley, some rosemary, a stalk of celery, a sprig of fresh sage, a few leaves of sweet basil, wrapping them in newspaper. These *odori*—or "odors"—are just the right balance of herbs for seasoning most any meat.

Herbs for seasoning are very important in Mediterranean cooking and are the difference between a plain and gourmet meal. An aura of mystery seems to surround an experienced Italian cook as he or she adds a branch of rosemary, a couple of cloves of garlic, a sprinkling of white or black pepper, several pinches of oregano, several leaves of basil, or *un pugno di prezzemolo*—"a fistful of parsley"—which can work wonders. Usually cultivated, sometimes wild, herbs are available for all those who wish to cook creatively.

Parsley, a biennial vegetable, is one of the most common herbs used in Italian cuisine. In the plant family, it is closely related to caraway. American parsley is very curly with crumpled green leaves. Italian parsley has broader, flat leaves. Parsley may be used fresh, dried, or frozen; it enhances flavor. Often casseroles and meats are garnished with fresh parsley to give color and flavor. Dieticians say parsley is a perfect complement to garlic, as its chlorophyll cancels garlic's strong odor. An excellent source of vitamins A and C, it is rich in iron and other minerals.

First grown in Sardinia and southern Italy, parsley was made into garlands by ancient Romans to crown the heads of military and athletic heroes. During funeral orations, parsley was passed through the audience and nibbled on during the services as breath fresheners.

*Father, thank you for the delight of various aromas and flavors that enhance
our lives and help make our human journey one of discovery and joy.*

Parsley grown indoors requires at least five hours of sunlight a day.

Spas

"Therefore with joy you will draw water From the wells of salvation."
Isaiah 12:3

From ancient times, Mediterranean people have enjoyed the spa or what they call, "taking the waters." Spa treatment is used to achieve three fundamental aims of medicine: prevention of illness, healing or convalescence, and maintenance of good health. Treatments include drinking mineral water, inhaling healing vapors, applications of hot mud, irrigation of the body, and warm-water exercise. Italian doctors consider spa treatment to be an important way to maintain health. A week or month's treatment at a spa is often prescribed by a physician and may be paid for by the nation's health department.

Different spas are known for their special water. Tuscany's Montecatini Terme was favored by Renaissance doctors who sent members of the Medici and Hapsburg-Lorraine families there for treatment. This popular spa's alkaline-sulfate waters are important for disorders of the liver, bile duct, stomach, and intestines. For treatment of liver ailments, a patient might go to Chianciano, another Tuscan spa.

At Fiuggi, east of Rome, waters rich in minerals are effective in the prevention and treatment of kidney stones. During the medieval papacy of Boniface VIII, couriers carried Fiuggi water to Rome for the pope's well being. In letters preserved in the British Museum, Michelangelo wrote of taking the waters of Fiuggi to his great benefit.

A local doctor discovered the therapeutic properties of the saline waters of Salsomaggiore near Parma in the early 19th century. This hot, artesian water contains high percentages of sodium chloride, bromine, and iodine and is good for many ailments. Nearby Tabiano Terme has sulfuric water, good for treating bronchial ailments.

The waters at Castellammare di Stabia near Naples contain sodium chloride. Ischia, an island southwest of Naples, is a holiday resort that has spas with curative, radioactive hot springs. The waters are said to heal female sterility and the mud baths relieve the pain of arthritis and rheumatism.

Creator of wonderful water, thank you for its healing, life-giving properties.

**Visitors will see the word *terme* in many spas' names;
it means "thermal bath."**

Ice Cream

*"Then I took the little book out of the angel's hand and ate it,
and it was as sweet as honey in my mouth.*
Revelation 10:10a

Italians claim to have invented ice cream. Emperor Nero is said to have kept his slave runners busy, bringing snow from distant mountains. His chefs quickly whipped up the snow with honey and fruit or wine. In Italy several decades ago, *gelato* was a summer specialty that disappeared like garden flowers when cool September breezes began blowing through her streets. Now, however, ice cream is a year-round treat in its native land. A *gelateria* offers several kinds of cones and cups of various sizes. A dollop of whipped cream is put on the cone or cup, if requested. One of Italy's favorite desserts is *macedonia di frutta con gelato* or "fresh fruit salad with vanilla ice cream."

Italy has many fantastic ice cream shops. The variety of flavors is always surprising. The ice cream is usually made in the shop, and every day there may be different flavors available. There are also yogurt, sherbet, and sugarless frozen treats. Aside from the usual chocolate, vanilla, and hazelnut, seasonal fresh fruit flavors may be available. Choose from cherry, sour cherry, strawberry, peach, apricot, plum, cantaloupe, watermelon, raspberry, blackberry, fig, persimmon, pear, prickly pear, apple, currant, muscat grape, concord grape, lemon, orange, tangerine, chestnut, pistachio, pineapple, coconut, or banana.

Summer tourists in Rome should go to the gelateria next to Ristorante Tre Scalini at Piazza Navona and order a *tartufo*, a ball of dark chocolate ice cream covered with grated bittersweet chocolate. Other fantastic frozen treats are *granita di caffè*, an almost frozen espresso coffee, and *granita di limone*, a slushy lemonade. The coffee ice is not sweetened but is spooned into a glass that has been lined with sweet whipped cream. The lemon ice is sharp and sweet and is served without whipped cream. Both of these ices can be purchased in most coffee bars and are guaranteed to make a person forget the heat of the most oppressive summer day.

Father, thank you for all the good things of life that give pleasure to our days.

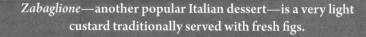

Zabaglione—another popular Italian dessert—is a very light
custard traditionally served with fresh figs.

Cold Drafts

"And the child grew. Now it happened one day that he went out to his father, to the reapers. And he said to his father, 'My head, my head!' So he said to a servant, 'Carry him to his mother.' When he had taken him and brought him to his mother, he sat on her knees till noon, and then died."

II Kings 4:18-20

Old-fashioned Italians may tell you that eating ice cream on a cold day can kill you. They advise against sudden changes of temperature, blasts of air on the back of the neck, or sitting near an open window. A sweating, straining day laborer wears a wool sweater in June because his mother told him when he was little he would die if he didn't. Many tall tales exist about deadly cold blasts.

One of the most famous of these Italian tales concerns Galileo Galilei when he was a young professor in Padua. On an extremely hot summer day, two of Galileo's friends asked him for a walk into the countryside where they thought they would be able to find a cool place. The three young men came upon the villa of the Count da Trento, who was a friend of the father of one of them.

The count was delighted to see his friend's son and the other young professors and suggested they rest in his large basement, which was naturally cool. He led them downstairs into a windowless room where a continuous, cool stream of air came from an underground cave. Comfortable chairs, cots, and lounges were placed around the basement room. The young men stretched out to rest, cooled off immediately, and fell asleep. Sometime later Galileo awoke with a burning throat, aching joints, and a strange sense of uneasiness. He staggered to his feet, stumbled to the doorway, shouted for help, and fainted.

Galileo was taken to Padua where attentive friends nursed him back to health. The other two young men died. Doctors said their bodies were overheated and then chilled too quickly by a sudden drop in temperature in the damp underground room. For the remainder of his life Galileo suffered from aches and pains that he attributed to this experience.

Loving Father, we thank you for seasons that help us to enjoy the great variety of earth's pleasures. Help us to enjoy the sun and warmth of summer.

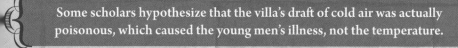

Some scholars hypothesize that the villa's draft of cold air was actually poisonous, which caused the young men's illness, not the temperature.

Regional Delights

"We remember the fish which we ate freely in Egypt, the cucumbers, the melons, the leeks, the onions, and the garlic; but now our whole being is dried up; there is nothing at all except this manna before our eyes!"
Numbers 11:5-6

When Elizabeth Taylor was asked how a trip to Italy was, she responded, "The pasta was wonderful!" Some tastes are so linked with location, they bear the names of those cities.

Rich pastas—such as *Spaghetti alla Bolognese*—served with lots of cheese, tomato sauce, and ground beef are in the manner of Bologna, which is also known for its processed meats.

Un fiorentino is a large, juicy beefsteak named for Florence, which also gives it name to pastas made with spinach and ricotta cheese such as *ravioli alla fiorentina*.

Fish or other dishes prepared *alla genoese*, from Genoa, are seasoned with pesto.

The city of Leghorn, or *Livorno* as Italians know it, excels in the preparation of fish—*pesce alla livornese*—serving it with a tomato sauce seasoned with onions, garlic, parsley, olive oil, white wine, salt, and pepper.

Cottaletta alla milanese, from Milan, is breaded veal cutlet. *Risotto alla milanese* is rice cooked with bright yellow saffron, a very expensive herb.

From Naples, *pizza alla napoletana* is topped with tomatoes, cheese, and anchovies. Neapolitan ice cream consists of layers of chocolate, strawberry, and vanilla ice creams. Anything labeled *alla romana* has tomatoes and herbs. Cooks in Rome's ghetto produced many Jewish specialties including *carciofi alla giudea* or artichokes stuffed with bread crumbs.

Fegato alla veneziana, from Venice, is calf or chicken liver cooked with onions and sage. And what Americans call a "Danish," Italians call a "Venetian." Enjoy *una veneziana*—a sweet roll—with your morning *caffè latte*.

Loving Father, help us to be open to the great variety of experiences life offers to us.

Sicilian cooks use many vegetables in their pasta dishes.

Wine

"He causes the grass to grow for the cattle, And vegetation for the service of man, That he may bring forth food from the earth, And wine that makes glad the heart of man, Oil to make his face shine, And bread which strengthens man's heart."

Psalm 104:14-15

For centuries people have avoided illness caused by contaminated water by drinking wine. Another reason wine is drunk with meals in Europe is that it counteracts the effect of olive oil. When we first moved to Italy, each delicious meal left my husband sick at his stomach. Soon a fellow diner advised him, "Signor Ruchti, you are in Italy where everything is cooked with olive oil. If you will drink a small glass of wine, you will have no digestive problems. Remember that Brother Paul advised young Timothy that 'A little wine is good for the stomach.'"

Every area of Italy has its special wine: Chianti near Orvieto, Lambrusco near Rome, Bardolino in northern Italy. For our first Thanksgiving in Italy, we went to Rivoli to celebrate with other Americans. As we drove through Umbria, we passed Montefiascone, on the edge of the Lake of Bolsena, where a miracle occurred. A German priest saw blood miraculously bathe the bread and wine of the mass. The miraculous host was taken to Orvieto where a great cathedral was built to enshrine it.

When traveling to Rome, Johannes de Fugger, Bishop of Augsburg, enjoyed good food and wine so much, he sent a servant ahead of him to sample local wines. When the servant found the best wine in the area, he wrote on the wall of the inn, *"Est,"* Latin for "It is." One day the servant arrived at Montefiascone, the Mountain of the Big Flask. The wine was deep red and very sweet and the best he had ever tasted. In his excitement, the servant wrote on the wall, *"Est, Est, Est!"* Fugger saw the endorsement and drank and drank; that night he died, contented. The bishop was buried in the Church of San Flaviano in Montefiascone. The translation of his tomb's inscription is: "On account of too much *Est Est Est* my master Johannes de Fugger died here." An extraordinary dessert wine, it's to die for!

We are grateful, Father, for all things that enrich our lives.

Italy makes twice as much red wine as white wine.

Olives

"But I am like a green olive tree in the house of God;
I trust in the mercy of God forever and ever.
Psalm 52:8

The olive tree is one of the longest-lived trees in the world. Some Italian olive groves have produced for centuries. Needing a hot, dry climate, the olive tree thrives around the Mediterranean Sea. They need hot, dry air when they flower and when the fruit develops. A certain amount of water is necessary but not too much or the roots will rot.

Italians take olives for granted. They enjoy green olives, black olives, small olives, large olives, olives cured in brine, olives cured in oil, olives seasoned with red peppers or capers, olives stuffed with pimento or anchovies. For supper, some farmers enjoy a plate of olives and a piece of bread, washed down with a glass of homemade wine. When olives are ripe, farmers spread large cloth or plastic sheets under their olive trees and shake the branches with long sticks. When they have shaken off all the ripe berries, they pick up the cloth and shake the olives into large baskets. Olive harvest usually comes between October and January.

The ripe fruit is purple to black and plum-shaped. Fresh olives are bitter and inedible and must be processed. They are shipped in barrels of light brine to processing plants where they are fermented a short time with lactic acid. Next they are given a lye bath and then washed to remove the bitter substance. Olives are darkened by exposure to air and then canned in brine or oil. Olives are graded according to size and quality. Green olives are a specialty of Spain and are processed differently. They aren't green because they were picked green but because of the curing process.

Creative God of the Universe, thank you for the variety
and abundance of your gifts to mankind.

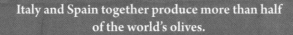

**Italy and Spain together produce more than half
of the world's olives.**

Olive Oil

*"For the LORD your God is bringing you into a good land, a land of brooks of water,
of fountains and springs, that flow out of valleys and hills; a land of wheat and barley,
of vines and fig trees and pomegranates, a land of olive oil and honey."*
Deuteronomy 8:7-8

Olive oil is basic to Italian cuisine, which is prized around the world. In Italy olives are grown primarily for their oil with the country producing almost three tons of olives annually. The flavor of the oil depends upon variety, ripeness, and age. If olives are picked green, the oil is bitter. If they are too ripe, the oil is rancid. "Virgin" olive oil is made from the first pressing of pulp and seeds. It is green and is never mixed with other oils.

In Italian food, the taste of olive oil is appreciated so much that oil and garlic are favorite garnishments for plain spaghetti—*spaghetti con aglio e olio*—and for toasted garlic bread or *bruschetta*. The basic Italian salad dressing is olive oil, vinegar, salt, and pepper. Italian cooks keep a can of olive oil by their stoves and pour it generously on pizzas, bread, and cooked vegetables. One of the favorite ways of serving green beans, spinach, or zucchini is to cook the vegetables, set them aside until they are room temperature, and then pour olive oil over the cold vegetables and serve. Some Americans gag at the sight of quantities of olive oil swimming around their veal or vegetables, but an Italian has a feeling of pleasure, as he breaks off a piece of bread, sops up the excess oil, and relishes the treat. Nutritionists say that olive oil is one of the most digestible of the edible fats.

Songs and poems and scripture remind us that olive trees were a constant part of the landscape of Palestine, as they were around the entire Mediterranean. Olives were used for medicine, food, and ritual holy oils. The Psalmist described the blessings of God: "You anoint my head with oil; My cup runs over" (23:5).

Creator God, thank you for blessing mankind with the olive tree.

The seed and flesh of an olive contains from 15 to 30 percent oil.

Nuts

"And their father Israel said to them, 'If it must be so, then do this: Take some of the best fruits of the land in your vessels and carry down a present for the man—a little balm and a little honey, spices and myrrh, pistachio nuts and almonds.'"
Genesis 43:11

Unless allergic, most people are nuts about nuts. In Italy nuts are sold on the streets in open markets, in shops that sell candied fruits and nuts, and in grocery stores.

The aroma of freshly roasting chestnuts, *castagne*, on a cold day is one of the first signs that winter has arrived. Vendors huddle over charcoal fires in small, portable metal braziers set up on sidewalks. They roast the chestnuts, turning them constantly to proper doneness. The vendor scoops a measure of roasted chestnuts into a paper cone that he has twisted into shape, which warms the customer's hands as he continues on his way. Candied chestnuts, sold in coffee bars and pastry shops, are available during winter months. Walnuts from Sorrento, *noce di Sorrento*, also are enjoyed as a dessert during winter.

Almonds, *mandorle*, are common to Italy. They are eaten green in early spring or are blanched, salted, toasted, or candy-coated. White, candy-coated almonds, *confetti*, are given with a small gift by a bride and groom to friends and relatives when they invite them to their wedding. Almonds also are given at births, baptisms, first communions, and wedding anniversaries.

The hazelnut, *nocciola*, is a favorite flavoring for ice cream and chocolate. Nutella, a hazelnut-chocolate cream, transforms a slice of bread into a special snack. Gianduia, a chocolate-hazelnut concoction, is decadently delicious. Baci, made in Perugia, are chocolate candy "kisses" with hazelnuts.

Ancient Romans believed pine nuts to be an aphrodisiac. They continue to be a standard ingredient in Italian cuisine and are often served with pesto sauce.

Pistachio ice cream, famous as an Italian specialty, is made with nuts imported from the Middle East. Brazil nuts are more common than pecans, queen of American nuts. In our home, Dub's raisin-walnut pie was a super substitute for pecan pie.

*Loving Lord, thank you for foods that nourish our bodies
and delight our senses.*

**Amedeo Obici, founder of Planters Peanut Company,
was born in Oderzo near Venice.**

Figs

"'In that day,' says the LORD of hosts, 'Everyone will invite his neighbor Under his vine and under his fig tree.'"
Zechariah 3:10

Fig leaves sewn together were the first clothes of Adam and Eve according to the Book of Genesis. Many references in the Bible reveal figs as a vital part of Mediterranean life. Before the third Punic War, the Roman senator Cato convinced the senate to protect itself from the Carthaginians on the north coast of Africa. During a speech to the senate, he held up a fresh fig and said, "Know this: this fig was picked only two days ago in Carthage. That's how close the enemy is to the walls of Rome." His words helped start the third Punic War in which Carthage was destroyed.

In front of the Curia in the Roman Forum a fig tree, an olive tree, and a grapevine grow close together. They are symbols and a tribute to these native Mediterranean plants that have contributed to the well-being of Rome. The ancients considered these plants to be special gifts to mankind. With these plants, plus wheat, an isolated community or farm could be self-sufficient with a sheep, cow, and chickens.

Italians eat fresh figs as a snack or as a dessert with knife and fork. As a summer appetizer, salty, crude ham from Parma and fresh figs—*prosciutto crudo e fichi*—are a delight for fig lovers.

Fresh figs do not last long or travel well but are easy to preserve by drying on large racks covered with gauzy cloth. Dried figs—rich in sugar, calcium, and iron—last for months. A favorite winter dessert, they are eaten alone or with nuts. A delicacy enjoyed in Calabria is fried fig pie or *nepitelle*. Figs are made into preserves and are also an ingredient in Christmas cakes. Lingering at the dinner table, eating figs, dates, and nuts while sipping a glass of wine, is an Italian custom on dreary winter Sunday afternoons.

Father, thank you for the abundant goodness and variety of your creation.

Planted in 288 B.C., the fig tree Sri Maha Bodhi in Sri Lanka is the oldest living human-planted tree.

Buon Natale

"For there is born to you this day in the city of David a Savior, who is Christ the Lord."
Luke 2:11

Buon Natale!—literally, "Good Christmas"—is the Italian holiday greeting that conveys the idea of the day's goodness and holiness. For centuries Christmas Day was a day set aside for the Christmas mass. During World War II, German, American, and British soldiers introduced the character Santa Claus.

On Christmas Eve churches in Italy are crowded for midnight mass. In Rome many people leave their own parish churches for Christmas mass with the pope at St. Peter's. Near each church's altar is a *presepio*, or a manger scene. It is complete except for the figure of the Baby Jesus. At midnight the baby is placed in the manger. Italians treasure their families' Christmas traditions of displaying their own manger scene in the living room, eating a hearty meal, and visiting relatives and friends. On many occasions, they enjoy *panettone*, a dome-shaped Christmas yeast bread with raisins and citron.

Traditionally, Christmas is celebrated for 12 days from December 25, the birth of Christ, to January 6, Epiphany or the coming of the Magi. Children receive gifts from *Befana*—a corruption of *Epifania*. Through hundreds of Christmases, the legend of Befana evolved. An old woman was sweeping her walk when Three Kings on camels stopped to ask directions to Bethlehem. She did not know the way and declined to go with them. Ever since Befana, carrying her broom, has given gifts to good children and lumps of coal to naughty ones on Epiphany.

Throughout days of preparation and celebration, the sights, smells, and sounds of Christmas please the senses. In Rome's Piazza Navona, Santa Claus and Befana hear the gift requests of children. Aromas of boiling candy and roasting chestnuts perfume the crisp, crackly air. Bag pipers from the Abruzzi Mountains play *Piva, Piva* and other wailing melodies that remind busy people that another blessed *Natale* is celebrated.

You came down from the stars, O King of Heaven, and came into a cave as cold as ice! O! How much it cost You to love me so! (Italian children's carol)

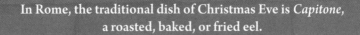

In Rome, the traditional dish of Christmas Eve is *Capitone*, a roasted, baked, or fried eel.

Italians

"I am a debtor both to Greeks and to barbarians, both to wise and to unwise. So, as much as is in me, I am ready to preach the gospel to you who are in Rome also."
Romans 1:14-15

The Italian personality is shaped by geography; influenced by history, politics, and religion; and dedicated to honoring the past and adapting to the challenges of the present. It would be impossible to describe exactly what an Italian is, or a Japanese, a Nigerian, or an American. There are too many different kinds of people in every country to arrive at a formula.

Some people see Italians as a noisy, happy, energetic people. Some people think they are negative and overcome by the burden of 3,000 years of history. George Bernard Shaw observed that in Italy everyone is an actor and the worst ones are on the stage. As a newcomer I was often the object of great curiosity in neighborhood stores. It seemed the onlookers created dramatic situations so they would have something to tell the family at the evening dinner table. Italian children are reared at the table. They grow up sitting on the laps of parents, grandparents, aunts, and uncles. They are held and kissed. They learn all the family stories and secrets of neighbors and friends. They learn to talk and listen simultaneously, to talk loud enough to be heard. They learn the joy of being with family and the value of a lazy Sunday afternoon. They learn early the importance of an afternoon nap, a walk, and time with friends.

Italians challenge others and respond to challenges. They learn to paint by watching an uncle. They learn to cook by helping *mamma*. Generally they do not speak quietly, except at a funeral. These self-assertive, intelligent, outgoing people host millions of foreigners each year. They absorb into their national citizenship thousands of people who marry Italians or move into their sun-blessed nation. During spring and summer they are overrun by tourists drawn to their sunny beaches and storied cities. The visitors will never be bored, for they are in the land of some of the most interesting people in the world—Italians—alive to life and to what it has to offer.

Thank you, Lord, for earth's great variety of people and places.

Italy is about the size of Georgia and Florida combined.

Section II
Historical Italy

Etruscans

"You are the light of the world. A city that is set on a hill cannot be hidden."
Matthew 5:14

While driving through Umbria and Tuscany at night, one sees jewel boxes of light in the distance, sparkling on black velvet hills. These hilltop towns were built so citizens could defend themselves against warring tribes. This area was known by Romans as Etruria, the land of the Etruscans. Etruscans were pre-Roman, their origins a mystery.

When Etruscans settled on the Italian peninsula at least 1,200 years before Christ, they became an advanced civilizing force. These newcomers brought with them wheeled carts and chariots, the use of iron, and writing with an alphabet. They cleared forests, drained swamps, and turned wild fields and groves into fertile gardens. They mined copper and iron. Their foundries manufactured large and small bronze items for artistic and utilitarian use. A peaceful people, Etruscans were dedicated to their crafts and to trade. They did not wage wars of expansion.

The first king of Rome was probably an Etruscan. Those creative people knew how to plan a city, to lay it out so its streets ran north and south, and to dedicate it properly so the gods would bless it. Etruscans were skilled in metallurgy and made useful and decorative pottery. They decorated their tombs with paintings and sculptures. Most of what we know about Etruscans we learn from their beautifully decorated tombs. Etruscan inscriptions are on tombs under the Roman Forum and elsewhere. An exact translation of their language is yet to be accomplished. Emperor Claudius Caesar was a student of Etruscan writings. After his death his life's work was destroyed and with it much knowledge about the people who taught the Romans how to be civilized.

Etruscans were the teachers of the Romans—the rugged Latin tribe, destined to rule the world.

Thank you, Father, for creativity in the work place. May our lives and our lights shine before men that they may see your glory.

German archeologist Werner Keller makes a good case for the Etruscans coming from Lydia in what is modern Turkey.

Romulus and Remus

"To all who are in Rome, beloved of God, called to be saints:
Grace to you and peace from God our Father and the Lord Jesus Christ."
Romans 1:7

Rome's origin lives in legend, shaped into history by Livy, whom Caesar Augustus asked to write Rome's history. Best known of all the stories about the Eternal City concerns her founding. Rhea Silvia, daughter of King Numitor, attended a sacred shrine and was ravished by a man who claimed to be Mars, god of war. To protect his reign, the king ordered his daughter's twin babies to be thrown into the Tiber River. Thinking the boys would drown, the king's servants put the babies in a basket and threw it into the river. But the basket floated and came to rest downstream on the riverbank. A thirsty she-wolf padded down from the hills to drink, heard the babies' hunger cries, and took them to her lair. The wolf suckled the human babies with her own, and they grew strong. A shepherd heard the babies crying, found them in the wolf's den, and took the boys home to his wife.

When the twin brothers—Romulus and Remus—grew up, they determined to establish their own city where the wolf den had been. On April 21, 753 B.C., they looked for signs from the gods in the flight of birds. From the Aventine Hill, Remus saw six vultures fly. But then a flight of 12 vultures flew over the Palatine Hill where Romulus stood watch. The brothers quarreled over the meaning; their supporters fought each other, and Romulus killed his brother and became the first king of Rome, the city he named for himself.

The wolf became the symbol of the city. Several ancient bronze statues of the wolf survive in Rome: on the Capitoline Hill, in Palazzo Venezia, and in the Vatican Museum. The suckling babies were added during the Renaissance.

Father, help us to learn the lessons of history from a culture begun in murder and rage. Help us to use your love and peace to obtain your purposes.

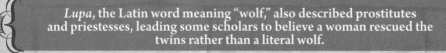

Lupa, the Latin word meaning "wolf," also described prostitutes and priestesses, leading some scholars to believe a woman rescued the twins rather than a literal wolf.

Center of the World

"Then the commander came and said to him, 'Tell me, are you a Roman?' He said, 'Yes.'
The commander answered, 'With a large sum I obtained this citizenship.' And Paul said,
'But I was born a citizen.'"
Acts 22:27-28

Pride in citizenship is the experience of most human beings. We are glad we are who we are. Orthodox Jew Paul of Tarsus was a citizen of Rome. More than once he used the power of his citizenship to save his life. At the Roman Forum, it is easy to imagine the pride of the average Roman at the time of Paul. Broken stones in today's Forum mark what was once the center of the Empire.

Originally, this land was a marshy trading place for Latin tribes 700 years before Christ. Modern archeologists, digging in the Roman Forum, found ruins of the original dwellings. The town of Rome, built on seven hills, grew and embraced the hills and valleys of Latium, and eventually the Italian peninsula. Five hundred years were necessary to bring all of Italy under Roman rule. Five hundred more years were needed to extend Rome's roads, language, law, and religion to include the civilized world. The Roman Empire extended from Portugal and Britain in the west to India in the east and the southern border of Scotland and the Rhine River in the north to the Sahara Desert in the south.

At the Forum the tourist sees the ruins of the center of the city, the center of the empire, the center of the world. "All roads lead to Rome," said the experienced travelers of the empire. On the western end of the Forum is the umbilicus—a small monument that indicates the place as being the navel of the empire. Mileage to any place in the empire was measured from that point. In God's good time mankind was readied for the coming of Messiah, His Son. The gospel was preached in a common language through the empire. Over an unparalleled system of roads, Christians carried their vibrant witness to cities and villages.

Father of all mankind, may we be good citizens of our
nation and your Kingdom.

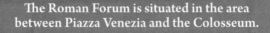

The Roman Forum is situated in the area
between Piazza Venezia and the Colosseum.

Castor and Pollux

"After three months we sailed in an Alexandrian ship whose figurehead was the Twin Brothers, which had wintered at the island."
Acts 28:11

The Twin Gods have several names. They were protectors of Rome and patron deities of sailors, wrestlers, and horse trainers. A figurehead of Castor and Pollux was on the brow of the ship that rescued Paul and others from the island of Malta. Born of the same mother, they were conceived on the same night by different fathers. Jupiter was the father of Pollux, who was therefore a god. King Tyndareus fathered Castor, a mortal.

According to mythology, Castor taught Hercules how to fight. The twins traveled with Jason on the Argo in his search for the Golden Fleece. After a storm on the sea, the Argonauts were filled with fear. Because the ship was saved miraculously, the twins were considered divine. From the beginning of the Roman Republic, Castor and Pollux were worshipped. In 496 B.C., during Rome's efforts to establish her rule around her seven hills, the Twin Gods helped the Romans in their battle against the Tarquins. Castor and Pollux announced the victory to the Romans. They watered their horses at the spring of Juturna near the Temple of Vesta. The Twins then disappeared immediately, as strangely as they had arrived.

In the Roman Forum stand the ruins of the Temple of Castor and Pollux, constructed near the spring where they watered their horses. Dedicated in 484 B.C., the temple was rebuilt by Tiberius in A.D. 19. The magnificent temple was standing when Paul arrived in Italy on the ship with the same name. Among ancient statues in Rome are the Twin Gods who stand with their horses in front of the president's palace on the Quirinal Hill. They have been a landmark for centuries. It is said these are among the few antique statues that were never covered by dirt and rubble.

Lord of the universe, as we journey through life,
give us guidance and protection.

The constellation Gemini is said to represent these twins. Its brightest stars, Castor and Pollux, are named for them.

Hannibal

"God is my strength and power, And He makes my way perfect."
II Samuel 22:33

During a sacrifice in a temple of Baal, Hamilcar Barcar—a general of Carthage—put his eight-year-old son Hannibal's hands on the head of a dead sheep on the altar and made him swear to resist the Romans all his life. Hannibal kept his oath, waging the Second Punic War.

Hannibal, 60,000 troops, and 37 African elephants crossed the Alps. Wagons and an animal pack train transported supplies. No army had ever made such a crossing over snow-covered peaks and rocky valleys. The huge elephants frightened the natives, scared the enemies' horses, and had to be coaxed over the cold, unfamiliar ground. The goal was Rome, which Hannibal had sworn to conquer. His purpose inspired his tired army.

Entering Italy, proud Hannibal claimed he had climbed Rome's walls. He pointed south to Italy's cities and invited his tired army to take for themselves its wealth—its meat, wine, fires, gold, and women. The alpine crossing had cost half the soldiers' lives. Hannibal and his army fought and wandered in Italy for 18 years with no new recruits except Italian people who had a quarrel with Rome. Hannibal's family in Carthage died of illnesses while he was away. At last, Hannibal fled to the protection of King Antiochus III of Syria and then to Bithynia, in what is now Turkey. When the Romans demanded his surrender, he committed suicide. He lived from 247 to 183 B.C.

When asked whom he thought was the greatest military leader in history, Hannibal answered, "Alexander the Great." But Hannibal's military tactics were so ingenious and successful they have been used by armies ever since. Places in Italy still bear the name of the Carthaginian general who gave the Romans fits. *Il Campo d'Annibale*, the Camp of Hannibal, is southeast of Rome at Rocca di Papa near the Italian Baptist youth camp.

Father, help us to learn how to cross the daunting barriers that complicate our lifelong struggles. May we have worthy goals for our lives.

Polybius, a Roman historian, wrote, "Of all that befell the Romans and the Carthaginians, the cause was one man, and one mind—Hannibal's."

Mars, the God of War

*"It happened in the spring of the year, at the time when kings go out to battle, that David
sent Joab and his servants with him, and all Israel … But David remained at Jerusalem."*
II Samuel 11:1

On the ancient Roman calendar, the first month of the year was named for Mars,
the god of war. The son of Juno, Mars was ranked second in power only to Jupiter and, unlike
his Greek counterpart Ares, was generally well-liked. He was believed to be the father of
Romulus, the first Roman, and his twin brother, Remus.

Mars delighted in battle and slaughter. Dressed in full armor, his helmet had a long
plume. He traveled at high speed in his war chariot drawn by four fiery steeds. Fierce dogs
and vultures accompanied him. The symbols of Mars were a spear and a burning torch. Mars
played a vital part in the legend of the fall of Troy, for he favored Paris who had captured the
beautiful Helen and taken her to Troy.

In Rome he was known as Mars Ultor or Mars the Avenger. The sacred spears of
Mars were kept with state archives and official records in the Regia, the house of the early
kings of Rome. Caesar Augustus built a temple to Mars Ultor to whom he attributed the
defeat of Brutus and Cassius at Philippi in 42 B.C., thus avenging the death of Julius Caesar,
and securing his accession to the throne. The Roman ensigns and the sword of Julius Caesar
were preserved in the Temple of Mars. Augustus also built a massive stone wall 100-feet
high to protect the Temple of Mars the Avenger from fire. Today only a few columns of the
temple stand in the Forum of Augustus. During the reign of Augustus, Mars rested, as the
Pax Romana was imposed on the world.

When the planets were named for the gods, the reddish planet, fourth from the sun,
was named for Mars, the bloody red god of war.

*Loving Lord, help us to live peacefully with all people. We pray for our world
and the many nations who are at war.*

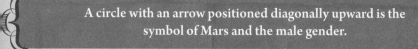

**A circle with an arrow positioned diagonally upward is the
symbol of Mars and the male gender.**

Julius Caesar's Rise to Power

"They shall speak of the glory of Your kingdom, And talk of Your power."
Psalm 145:11

"O Julius Caesar, thou art mighty yet!" says Brutus in the last act of Shakespeare's epic tragedy. Gaius Julius Caesar ruled Rome from 49 to 44 B.C. Born in Rome to an aristocratic family, Julius Caesar was well educated as a boy. At 17 he married Cornelia, daughter of a Roman aristocrat. When Sulla, dictator of Rome, ordered Caesar to divorce Cornelia, he refused. Forced to leave Rome, he went to Greece to study philosophy and oratory. His clear thoughts and facility with words, whether written or spoken, made his ideas powerful tools.

Pardoned by Sulla, Caesar returned to Rome where he became involved in public affairs. In 65 B.C. he was elected director of public works and games. Appealing to the self-indulgence of the idle Romans, he borrowed heavily to provide lavish spectacles of animal fights and gladiatorial combats to entertain and win the favor of the people. In 60 B.C., Caesar, Crassus, and Pompey formed the First Triumvirate, the rule of Rome by three men, all successful generals.

Knowing that military victories would give him political fame, Caesar displayed his military genius and seemed almost invincible, losing only two battles in nine years. He expanded the Roman territory to the Rhine River. Twice he invaded Britain, the Wild West of the Roman Empire. Pompey was alarmed at Caesar's success and ordered Caesar to give up his army. But Caesar was too shrewd and ambitious to leave his army unprotected. Marching toward Rome near the Adriatic Sea, he crossed the small Rubicon River that separated his provinces from Italy.

A struggle for power was inevitable. Pursuing Pompey to Greece, Caesar defeated him the following spring at the battle at Pharsalus. Julius Caesar was then the master of Italy.

Father, Yours is the kingdom, the power, and the glory.
We submit ourselves to you, our maker, our Lord.

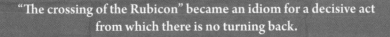

"The crossing of the Rubicon" became an idiom for a decisive act
from which there is no turning back.

Veni, Vidi, Vici

*"Render therefore to Caesar the things that are Caesar's,
and to God the things that are God's."*
Matthew 22:21b

"I came, I saw, I conquered," wrote Caesar of a military victory in northwestern Turkey. Everywhere he went, he was victorious, and his enemies hated him for it. To test popular feelings for Caesar, Mark Anthony offered him a crown three times before a Roman crowd. Knowing the Roman hatred of kings, Caesar refused the crown, though the crowd urged him to take it.

In his 56 years of life, this intelligent, shrewd general left his mark on the Mediterranean world and on Europe by his military battles. He worked to unify the empire and to give full Roman citizenship to all free men within the empire. He created new cities to give the landless poor an opportunity for a good life. He had a census taken in Italy, built a great public library, rebuilt the Forum, reformed coinage and the calendar, and ordered vast public works all over the empire. His detailed diaries became textbooks for generations of school children.

A group of jealous senators plotted to kill Julius Caesar on March 15, 44 B.C. He had been warned by a soothsayer, "Beware the Ides of March," the middle of the month. Despite the warning, Caesar went to the Theatre of Pompey for the day's meeting of the Senate, because the Senate building was being repaired. So no one person could be identified as Caesar's murderer, the plotting senators who surrounded him stabbed him 20 times. He fell at the foot of the statue of Pompey, which today stands in Palazzo Spada.

Julius Caesar was buried in the Roman Forum near the House of the Vestal Virgins, though by law only Vestal Virgins could be buried within the city walls. His family name, "Caesar" became so closely associated with the idea of emperor, it became a title. Even in the days of the Byzantine Empire, more than 300 years later, any national ruler could be called Caesar.

*Our Father, may our own actions, attitudes, and ambitions
be in accord with your will for us.*

The title "Caesar" is *Czar* in Russian and *Kaiser* in German.

Cicero

"A word fitly spoken is like apples of gold In settings of silver."
Proverbs 25:11

Friends visiting from Georgia wanted to see the Villa of Cicero at the ruins of Tusculum. Situated on the top of a hill, Tusculum commands a view of surrounding hills, especially dramatic at sunset. After walking through the ruins of the Villa of Cicero, the theater, and some other stone ruins, we set up our picnic table on the crest of the hill and ate supper, while enjoying the sunset, the gathering twilight, and the twinkling lights of the hilltop towns of Lazio.

Marcus Tullius Cicero was born in 106 B.C., son of a wealthy family. He studied law, oratory, Greek literature, and philosophy in Rome and Greece. He became a lawyer and had a political career as praetor and then consul. He believed strongly in a republican government and dedicated his life to preventing the dying Roman Republic from turning into a dictatorship.

Cicero's outspokenness caused some nobles to dislike him. He refused to join in the First Triumvirate in 60 B.C. As a result, he was banished from Rome. Julius Caesar and Cicero were reconciled after Pompey's defeat, but later Cicero approved of—but did not participate in—Caesar's murder. Afterward he was the unofficial leader of the Senate where he gave more than 14 speeches against Mark Antony, blaming him for many of Rome's problems. His enmity with Antony led to his downfall, and he was assassinated in 43 B.C. as he tried to escape from Tusculum.

Cicero's eloquent orations are among the most studied Latin writings. He wrote essays on philosophy, political theory, theology, and oratory. More than 1,000 of his letters survive. Modern writers find in his speeches the model for constructing a persuasive speech. He Latinized Greek words to better express philosophical ideas, expanding the vocabulary for his use and for the future.

Father, thank you for giving us tongues to sing your praise and to communicate with others. Help us to use our words wisely and for the good of others.

One of Cicero's most important cases was defending the people of Sicily against their robber-governor. Eventually, he obtained Roman citizenship for Sicilians.

Roman Roads

"And so we went toward Rome. And from there, when the brethren heard about us, they came to meet us as far as Appii Forum and Three Inns. When Paul saw them, he thanked God and took courage."

Acts 28:14b-15

Most people have heard the maxim, "All roads lead to Rome." Actually, 19 roads entered Rome. These roads joined the 372 imperial roads to link the Roman Empire with a 53,000 mile network of stone. Roman roads extended from Hadrian's Wall at the boundary between England and Scotland to India. They were built as directly as possible from the Pillars of Hercules (Gibraltar) on the Mediterranean Sea to the Temple of the God Terminus on the Euphrates River. They linked the empire through the deserts of North Africa to the forests of Germany.

In his book *The Roads That Led to Rome*, Victor W. Van Hagen says, "The most enduring monuments are those ubiquitous, those overwhelming Roman roads. It is the massive grandeur of these stone-laid highways which lead out to the most remote horizons which is Rome's monument."

Usually roads were built at the command of an emperor or leader who also might finance their construction. Designed by architects and engineers of great skill, roads were built by large groups of prisoners, slaves, or soldiers. When Rome was at peace, soldiers often spent their days building roads instead of fighting barbarians.

When the traveler arrived at the gates of Rome, he was required to leave his cart, chariot, or horse and proceed on foot. Julius Caesar had proclaimed that from sunrise until sunset there would be no cart, wagon, chariot, or any form of transport moving within the precincts of Rome. For more than 400 years, that proclamation was law, meaning all deliveries were made during the night. "And so we came to Rome," ends the book of Acts, which relates Paul's journeys over the many roads he traveled to preach the good news of Jesus Christ. He entered Rome on the famous, enduring Appian Way.

Lord, guide us in our journeys as we seek to follow your way.

Throughout Europe, the Middle East, and North Africa, there are parts of some Roman roads that are still in use after 2,000 years.

Cleopatra

"Do not devise evil against your neighbor, For he dwells by you for safety's sake."
Proverbs 3:29

Beautiful, brilliant, witty, seductive, ruthless, and scheming, one of the most famous women in history became involved with two Roman leaders in her efforts to restore the power of Egypt. When Ptolemy XI died in 51 B.C., Cleopatra and her 10-year-old brother, Ptolemy XII, were made joint rulers. After two years, her brother's guardians seized power and drove Cleopatra from the throne.

The following year Julius Caesar arrived in Alexandria in pursuit of Pompey. He fell in love with the charming Cleopatra when he met her in the palace. In the civil war that followed, Cleopatra's brother was defeated and killed. A younger brother, Ptolemy XIII, then shared the throne with Cleopatra. She went to Rome with Caesar and their son, Caesarion, in 46 B.C. and stayed until Caesar's assassination in 44 B.C. Upon her return to Egypt, she ordered her brother put to death so she could share the throne with her son, who took the name Ptolemy XIV.

In 41 B.C. after Mark Anthony and Octavian defeated Brutus and Cassius at Philippi, it was decided Mark Antony would rule the eastern part of the empire. While at Tarsus in Asia Minor, preparing for war against the Parthians to the east, Mark Antony met with Cleopatra. He deserted his wife and married Cleopatra in 37 B.C. They conspired together for him to be sole ruler of Rome, using the wealth of Egypt to help him gain power. She wanted Egypt to be a partner in empire, not a conquered province. In 31 B.C. Octavian defeated Anthony in the naval battle of Actium near Greece. Believing Cleopatra dead, Mark Anthony committed suicide. A few days later, Cleopatra killed herself with the help of a deadly asp. After her death, Caesarion was executed. Egypt was a conquered province to be pillaged of its goods.

Loving Lord, help us to be honest in our dealings with others.

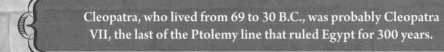

Cleopatra, who lived from 69 to 30 B.C., was probably Cleopatra VII, the last of the Ptolemy line that ruled Egypt for 300 years.

Augustus Caesar

"And it came to pass in those days that a decree went out from Caesar Augustus that all the world should be registered."
Luke 2:1

"Meet me at the Tomb of Caesar Augustus!" Romans say. Near the center of downtown Rome are the ruins of Caesar's tomb. He was an emperor-god and thus entitled to a tomb within the city walls. On one side of the tomb is a busy bus stop, on another the very popular Alfredo's Restaurant. Close by is the Altar of Peace, built to celebrate 100 years of *Pax Romana*, or Roman Peace, that began with the reign of Augustus.

Octavian was the original name of Augustus, adopted son of Julius Caesar. In his will, Julius named Octavian his heir, but in order to secure the throne for himself, Octavian had to defeat the armies of Mark Anthony because there was no tradition of an inherited throne. Then together Octavian and Anthony led an army against their enemies, Brutus and Cassius, who had murdered Julius. A battle at Philippi in Greece in 42 B.C. established Octavian as ruler of the western provinces and Anthony as ruler of the eastern provinces.

In 27 B.C. Octavian was named emperor after defeating Anthony in battle. Such great peace descended on the empire that the Senate voted the name Augustus, meaning "the exalted one," for Octavian and gave him power to direct religious, civil, and military affairs. He ruled peacefully for 41 years and maintained an honest government, free trade among the provinces, a sound currency system, an efficient postal system, and improved harbors while also establishing new colonies. It has been said of him, "He found Rome brick and left it marble," because of his reputation of outstanding accomplishment for the glory of the empire and the well-being of its citizens.

Augustus played a part in divine prophecy when he ordered the census. Joseph and Mary were required to register in their ancestral home in Judea, and there Jesus was born in Bethlehem, the city of their ancestor, King David.

Lord God, we pray for our political leaders whose decisions affect our daily lives and our future. May there be honesty and integrity in the halls of power.

After his death in A.D. 14, the Senate voted Augustus Caesar
the title, "The Divine Augustus."

Tiberius Caesar

"After these things Jesus went over the Sea of Galilee, which is the Sea of Tiberias. Then a great multitude followed Him, because they saw His signs which He performed on those who were diseased."
John 6:1-2

"Tiberio's Restaurant" was the name of an Italian restaurant in Rome, Georgia, owned by a Capri native living there. Why Tiberio? *Tiberio* is the Italian equivalent for Tiberius, son of Livia, third wife of Augustus Caesar. Tiberius was adopted by the emperor and grew up to be a successful army commander. Caesar Augustus considered Tiberius as a possible heir to the throne, as several other successors had died. Some speculate Livia was behind these political assassinations as she wanted her son to follow Augustus as emperor.

Tiberius became emperor in A.D. 14. He was a good and serious administrator, supervising tax collections and balancing the budget. He chose efficient governors and hoped to put society right and restore the ancient moral qualities of Rome. But Romans didn't care for an emperor-reformer who didn't enjoy the games of the arena. They wanted to be entertained, and Tiberius interfered with their vulgar diversions. Whereas Julius Caesar and Augustus Caesar had used the games to demonstrate their power and the power of Rome, Tiberius rarely attended. Trying to economize, he set a strict budget for public spectacles, lowered the pay of performers, and reduced the number of gladiatorial combats at a given festival.

Pampered Romans hated his economies and regretted the loss of the extravaganzas of days past. When Tiberius refused to allow senators and members of knightly classes to appear in the arena, Romans thought of him as a prude. The strong public dislike and his private grief—due to a forced divorce of his first beloved wife and the deaths of his sons—caused him to move to Campania, near Naples. Later, he moved to Capri where the ruins of the Villa of Tiberius are still a sight to see.

Merciful God, help us to honor you through our choices, actions, and lives.

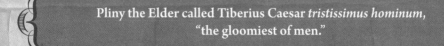

Pliny the Elder called Tiberius Caesar *tristissimus hominum*, "the gloomiest of men."

Gladiators

"You shall not murder."
Exodus 20:13

Gladioli, brightly colored flowers on a long stem with sword-shaped leaves, are sold in Italy's flower stalls. The gladiolus, often nurtured in greenhouses, can be bought all year. The sword-shaped leaves that give the plant its name are related to the Latin word for sword, *gladius*. That same word gives us *gladiator*, or "one who uses a sword." Romans learned from the Etruscans to play these deadly games, originally performed as funeral rites.

Gladiators were slaves, prisoners of war, convicted criminals, or individuals who fought for riches and short-lived glory. According to historian Jerome Carcopino, weapons were varied. Some gladiators used a two-foot-long sword, a long shield, and a visored helmet. Others used a short, curved scimitar or sword, and a short, round shield called a buckler. Still others used a net and a three-pronged spear called a trident. Sometimes the battle was a mock one, fought with muffled weapons, as fencing matches are staged with buttons on the foils. This type of fight filled the program for days and was a warm-up for the real fights.

A series of duels, or *munus*, was common: the gladiator escaped death only by killing his opponent. Sometimes only gladiators of the same category fought each other while other times people fought wild animals. In A.D. 90 during the reign of Domitian, the crowds were titillated when a dwarf was pitted against a female gladiator.

This type of torture became useful in disposing of Christians of the early church. A favorite legend concerns a company of Roman soldiers who were commanded to swear allegiance to the emperor. Instead of saying, "Caesar is Lord!" they hailed their Savior, declaring: "We are soldiers, fighting for Thee, oh Lord, for Thee to win the victor's crown. Jesus Christ is Lord!" For their treason, they were butchered in the arena.

Father of all, help us to grasp the simple truth that all of earth's creatures are precious in your sight and are to be treated with respect and care.

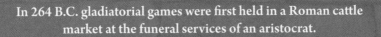

In 264 B.C. gladiatorial games were first held in a Roman cattle market at the funeral services of an aristocrat.

Little Boot

"The fear of the LORD is the beginning of knowledge,
but fools despise wisdom and instruction."
Proverbs 1:7

His father's soldiers nicknamed him *Caligula*, which means "Little Boot," for as a child he cockily wore military boots. Born Caius Caesar Augustus Germanicus, when he became emperor he was known by his childhood nickname. Great grandson of Augustus Caesar, Caligula was the son of Germanicus and Agrippina the Elder. In Roman tradition, Caligula was adopted by his uncle, Tiberius Caesar, and became emperor when he died in A.D. 37. Vile and sensuous, he had unnatural relations with his three sisters, one of whom he may have murdered. Many deaths in the imperial house and among the aristocracy were attributed to him. Common people were of no more value to him than garbage.

At the beginning of his reign, however, Caligula seemed to have had noble intentions and gave the impression that he wished to put right the abuses of Tiberius' last, weak years. He published the imperial budget, recalled exiles, lowered taxes, had judges reinstated. But he had a mania that destroyed him: an obsession to be liked. He was willing to do anything for applause. Caligula began buying the gratitude of the people by providing free shows, performed at night and all day in the circus. He lived for the excitement of the arena and for the applause of the crowds when he spoke to them from the emperor's box.

Little Boot said he wished all Romans had one neck so he could execute them all at once. Robert Graves in *I, Claudius* described the madness that consumed the emperor. Caligula believes he is becoming a god. Fumbling, bumbling Claudius humors Caligula and tells him his face is shining. Caligula asks for a mirror and sees a godly glow. From that moment Caligula begins to plot ways to prove he is superior to others. He had the power of their lives in his hands.

Father, help us to learn from evil men so we do not imitate their lust for power.

Caligula himself met death in the arena. During an intermission at one of his shows, he was stabbed to death by an unidentified assailant.

Roman Soldiers

"If a soldier demands that you carry his gear for a mile, carry it two miles."
Matthew 5:41 (NLT)

Jesus had seen Roman soldiers. Maybe he had talked with them and carried their gear as he walked along the roads of Galilee and Judea. Throughout the Roman Empire, soldiers were a common sight. During the republic the army was composed of citizens who served in time of war. By the reign of Julius Caesar, most soldiers were professionals in a standing army. As the empire grew, the need for an army grew. By the time of Augustus Caesar the army numbered about 250,000 men.

The Roman army was an organization composed of units or divisions called legions. In various periods of Roman history, a legion consisted of 4,000 to 6,000 men. A general commanded each legion, which were divided into six military tribunes. Sixty centurions each led a century, a unit of 100 men. Legions were also divided into cohorts of 550 fighters. Compulsory military training of all citizens kept the legions filled. New soldiers were hardened by intense training and were drilled until they reacted as a mechanical unit to orders from their superior. Several centurions mentioned in the gospels were God-seekers, admirable people.

Each legion had a standard—an eagle of silver or gold—which was carried at the front. It was carried high so soldiers would know where their cohort was. If the soldier holding it was struck in battle, someone else picked up the standard so its presence would continue to encourage the fighting men.

Legionnaires marched to battle. They carried their weapons, their entrenching tools with which to make camp, their food, and their tents. They had the legal right to compel the conquered inhabitants of the empire to help with their heavy loads.

Lord, help us to be willing to help others with their burdens and their problems.

So efficient in battle was the trained Roman legion that the Gauls
said it was the gift of the war god, Mars, to the Latin tribes.

Claudius, the Stuttering Prince

"To everything there is a season, A time for every purpose under heaven:
A time to keep silence, And a time to speak."
Ecclesiastes 3:1, 7b

After the death of Caligula in A.D. 41, the most unlikely candidate for the office of emperor was Claudius. Born in Lyons, he was named Tiberius Claudius Drusus. When his brother was adopted into the Julian family, he added the surname Germanicus to his own name.

Claudius was subject to many slights, which today would be called child abuse. If he arrived late to supper, he was forced to walk around the room several times before he was permitted to sit. Often he went to sleep at the end of meals, stretched out on a sofa by the table. The family enjoyed playing pranks on him, throwing olive stones and dates at him. Sometimes they put slippers on his hands as he lay snoring. When he awoke, he rubbed his face with the slippers, and everyone laughed. His mother, Antonia, was repulsed by his presence. She often called him "an imperfect man, whom nature had begun but had not finished." When she wished to insult someone, she would say, "He is a greater fool than my son Claudius."

He turned to academic research to retain his sense of dignity and sanity. More than any scholar of his day, Claudius became an authority on the Etruscan language and history. But his monumental work of 50 volumes was destroyed after his death because some thought his discoveries detracted from Rome's claims of accomplishments. Claudius had never been allowed to hold public office except when his nephew, Caligula, became emperor.

Some historians think that for his life's sake Claudius pretended to be half-witted. He had a stuttering problem and constantly jerked his head when he talked. When he was about to be made emperor, his sister Livilla loudly expressed her indignation that the Roman people should experience a fate so severe and so much below their grandeur. No one had any idea that the clumsy, stuttering fool would become one of Rome's greatest emperors.

Father, make us as wise as serpents and as harmless as doves when we must
protect ourselves from evil forces.

Claudius was the first Roman emperor to be born outside Italy.

Claudius Caesar

"After these things Paul departed from Athens and went to Corinth. And he found a certain Jew named Aquila, born in Pontus, who had recently come from Italy with his wife Priscilla (because Claudius had commanded all the Jews to depart from Rome);
and he came to them."
Acts 18:1-2

When Claudius was 50 years old, Caligula was assassinated. Afraid he would be killed next, Claudius hid on a balcony behind door curtains. A passing soldier saw his feet under the curtains, pulled him out, and immediately recognized him. The soldier threw himself at the feet of the royal stutterer and saluted him, "Emperor!" The next day when the senate met and did not know who to appoint emperor, citizens shouted they would have Claudius as their leader. Claudius allowed the armed guards to swear allegiance to him. He promised them 15,000 sesterces each for their loyalty, becoming the first emperor to purchase the submission of soldiers with money.

Claudius was a capable ruler. For the increasing responsibilities of the empire, he formed a civil service system that placed specialized bureaus in charge of various branches of government. The Claudian Aqueduct still stands in the Roman countryside. In addition to increasing Rome's water supply, he had unhealthy marshland drained. One of the great engineering feats of the time was the dredging and enlarging of the harbor at Ostia, the port of Rome. He was called Claudius Britannicus because he conquered parts of Britain, as far as Scotland. He added Thrace, now the Balkan Peninsula, to the empire.

Claudius had several unhappy and unfortunate marriages. His third wife, Messalina, was notorious for her scandalous affairs. She and her lover were executed by Claudius' freedmen who feared for the life of their master. His last wife, Agrippina, was his niece. The mother of Nero, she urged Claudius to adopt her son, who had married the daughter of Claudius. So Nero, the son-in-law, became adopted son and heir to the throne. Soon after Agrippina made the arrangements for Nero to succeed him, Claudius died in A.D. 54 in the 14th year of his reign. Agrippina is believed to have arranged his murder.

Father, help us learn to live in harmony with your will.

Olive oil cost about two to three sesterces per quart.

Nero

"Now to Him who is able to keep you from stumbling, And to present you faultless Before the presence of His glory with exceeding joy, To God our Savior, Who alone is wise, Be glory and majesty, Dominion and power, Both now and forever. Amen."
Jude 1:24-25

His name means "black," and he is remembered as the black-hearted leader who persecuted Christians. The last Roman emperor related to the Caesars, Nero was proclaimed emperor several hours after the assassination of his adoptive father, Claudius, in A.D. 54.

Nero was a good musician and an effective administrator, delegating responsibilities to capable people. After a revolt in Britain, he brought peace to the province. He sent a fleet to protect Roman ships and commerce on the Black Sea. For wars in Armenia and Judea he chose excellent military commanders. He applied Roman law, even when it seemed unjust. Tired of his mother's interference, he had her murdered in A.D. 59. Three years later he had his first wife killed to marry Poppaea Sabina.

Rome's most famous fire began near Circus Maximus between the Palatine and Caelian hills. The city was ravaged, and its food supplies destroyed. Nero's own palace burned. To relieve the homeless, Nero opened to them Mars Field, the public buildings of Agrippa, and his own gardens. He had temporary shelters built for the people. From neighboring towns food was brought and then sold to the public at reduced prices.

Despite all the emperor did, Romans thought Nero had ordered the city's burning. To exonerate himself, Nero blamed the Christians whose teachings were new and different. He ordered that Christians be dipped in tar and set on fire in his garden. Some Christians were killed in the Circus of Nero and Caligula on Vatican Hill. Tradition says both Peter and Paul were executed during Nero's reign. A year later when a plot was formed to assassinate him, he fled from Rome. Four miles north of the city in the suburban villa of one of his freedmen, Nero committed suicide in A.D. 68. The people rejoiced.

Loving Father, help us to learn that we cannot make the rules for moral living. Help us to submit ourselves to your simple laws that enable us to have happy lives.

Nero became emperor at 16, the youngest ruler yet.

Slavery

"I appeal to you to show kindness to my child, Onesimus. I became his father in the faith while here in prison … He is no longer like a slave to you. He is more than a slave, for he is a beloved brother, especially to me. Now he will mean much more to you, both as a man and as a brother in the Lord."

Philemon 1:10, 16 (NLT)

Can you imagine being owned by someone else? From early times slavery has existed. During the Roman Empire, the institution of slavery became entrenched to such a degree that an immediate abolition of slavery would have destroyed the empire and its infrastructure. As the empire grew, more and more people were enslaved. In the second century B.C., a Roman family might have one slave. By the second century A.D., most homes had at least two slaves. Julius Caesar owned approximately 20,000.

Not only were captives of war made slaves, but innocent people captured by pirates were forced into galleys or sold at slave auctions. Sometimes destitute parents sold their children into slavery so they could pay their debts. Uneducated slaves were farm workers or workers in mines. Condemned criminals were sent to the salt mines or to the galleys.

Though slaves had no legal rights, surprisingly some of the finest teachers in the empire were slaves from Greece or Alexandria. Many illiterate or poorly educated Roman citizens bought themselves a Greek who took care of his master's complicated business affairs. Freed of these details, the less-educated master enjoyed the public games, bathhouses, elaborate banquets, and his house in the country. Some educated slaves were treated like free men. Many noble Romans entrusted their business to their educated slaves to such an extent that the upper classes were subject to the decisions of the slaves of the rulers. The tutor, doctor, or scribe often enjoyed close contacts with the master and his family. Many slaves, however, only knew lives of hunger, misery, and crushing labor.

But the climate of the empire was right for the Pauline teaching that in Christ there is neither bond nor free. Masters and slaves worshipped together in house churches during the first centuries of the Christian era. These socially and politically unequal Christians accepted fellow believers as brothers and sisters in the faith. Slavery was doomed.

Father of all, we pray that all nations will be free of slavery.

It is estimated that more than 25 percent of the population of Ancient Rome was enslaved.

Vespasian

"For we are God's fellow workers; you are God's field, you are God's building."
I Corinthians 3:9

Four emperors followed Nero's rule in A.D. 69: Galbus, Otho, Vitellius, and finally Vespasian. A 60-year-old widowed general, Vespasian was a man of the people. One of his first decisions was to give back to the Roman people the land Nero had seized for his Golden House. He drained the ornamental lake in Nero's garden and built the colossal Flavian Ampitheater, the official name of the Colosseum. He wanted Rome to be the trading and financial center of the world, the visible expression of the greatness of the Roman Empire.

In the Colosseum, Vespasian attempted what Augustus planned but never started, what Caligula started but abandoned, and what Nero rejected because he was content with a wooden amphitheater.

Vespasian restored order to the city and repaired the financial structure of the empire after Caligula's and Nero's senseless extravagances. A tax collector's son, he knew the power of money and the necessity of raising it. He is remembered as the emperor who taxed the latrines of Rome. When Titus, heir to the throne, said this was unworthy of the emperor, Vespasian handed him a coin, the first of the new tax, and asked, "Does it smell, my son?" A great builder, Vespasian rebuilt many of the buildings destroyed by Nero's fire. As an example to the citizens, he carried the first basketful of rubble to begin restoring the Capitol. Three columns remain of the Temple of Vespasian that was built in his honor in the Forum.

In A.D. 79 Vespasian was succeeded by Titus, the general who had destroyed Jerusalem in A.D. 70. The impressive Arch of Titus in the Forum honors that victory. Domitian succeeded his brother Titus. He tried to restore the pagan religion. He built the Circus of Domitian, the area that is now known as Piazza Navona. During his reign Christians, Jews, and others were persecuted. He was assassinated in A.D. 96.

Creator of the universe, Help us to use our strength and creativity
to develop a wholesome society.

In colloquial Italian, a *vespasiano* is a street urinal.

Days and Weeks

In the book of Genesis we read that God created the world in six days and rested on the seventh. The Hebrews considered seven days as a basic division of time. Four weeks made a month, the length of the moon's cycle. But the Roman world saw in the seven movable stars, including the sun and moon, the powers of fate presiding over the hours and days. In Mediterranean cultures, the first day of the week honored the conquering sun god, Apollo; second, the moon goddess, Diana; third, Mars; fourth, Mercury; fifth, Jupiter; sixth, Venus; and seventh, Saturn.

Romans believed that the gods were active on their special day. Saturn, for instance, was a very mischievous god, so Saturday was a day for indulging oneself in pleasure. The seven days of the week were all workdays. There was no weekly day of rest, though there were numerous holidays—or holy days—throughout the year. To celebrate pagan holy days, people went to the temples and offered sacrifices. Shops were closed, and work stopped. On festival days, free men abstained from lawsuits, and slaves rested from work.

The early Christian church in the Roman Empire worshipped on the first day of the week instead of observing the Jewish Sabbath at the end of the week. Because Christ had risen from the dead on the first day of the week, they soon established Sunday as the day to remember the resurrection. About the middle of the second century, Justin Martyr explained the Christian day of worship by saying that the first day is "the day of light," which recalls the creation, and the fact that Christ, "the true sun," rose from the darkness of the grave on the first day of the week. This explanation confused the pagans, who thought Christians were honoring the sun.

Father, we thank you for days to work and nights to rest,
for the movement of the universe. May we use each day for your glory.

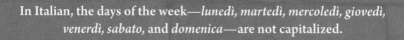

In Italian, the days of the week—*lunedì, martedì, mercoledì, giovedì, venerdì, sabato,* and *domenica*—are not capitalized.

Diana and the Temple at Nemi

"They shall fear You As long as the sun and moon endure, Throughout all generations."
Psalm 72:5

One summer day a friend and I took our daughters on an outing to the ruins of the Temple of Diana, which had stood in the woods overlooking Lake Nemi. A kind farmer showed us some of the fragments of the temple and indicated its dimensions. Long ago most of the stone and marble was recycled into the buildings of the town of Nemi, which is located on the rim of an extinct volcano.

Diana, virgin goddess of the moon, was the daughter of Jupiter. Dressed in white, she wore silver sandals and carried a silver bow. She was a friend to mortals and protected wild animals. Also goddess of the hunt, Diana is often depicted with a hound or boar. At night she rode her silver chariot across the sky and shot her arrows of moonlight to the earth below. She was goddess of fertility, childbirth, and of wild woodlands. Worshipped throughout the Roman world, her temple in Ephesus was one of the seven wonders of the ancient world. In Acts 19, there is an account of a riot in Ephesus when Demetrius, a silversmith, warned the Ephesians that the preaching of Paul would bring about the end of the worship of Diana.

The town of Nemi was founded in 321 when the temple ceased to exist. Today Nemi is a picturesque and popular holiday resort. It is only 21 miles from Rome and accessible by car or bus. Delightful walking paths are along the sides of the ancient crater. Many different noble families ruled and enlarged the castle. The Ruspoli family became the owners in 1902. At the outbreak of World War II, Princess Eugenia Ruspoli, a native of Rome, Georgia, shipped the best antique furniture, paintings, and sculptures fom the castle to her sister, Martha Berry. These treasures are now on display at Berry College in Georgia.

We thank you, Father Creator, for sunshine and moonlight
and for your love for us.

Lake Nemi is also known as Diana's Mirror.

A Good Emperor

"All Your garments are scented with myrrh and aloes and cassia, Out of the ivory palaces,
by which they have made You glad. Kings' daughters are among Your honorable women;
At Your right hand stands the queen in gold from Ophir."
Psalm 45:8-9

Spanish by birth, Hadrian is known as one of the five good emperors. He reigned from 117 to 138. Educated in Rome, he fought with distinction along the Danube River frontier. He was made consul of Rome and for a time was a ruler of Athens. When Emperor Trajan—his ward since the childhood death of his father—died, the army and Roman Senate proclaimed Hadrian the new emperor.

At the time, the peace of the empire was threatened by revolts of its conquered people and by barbarian invasions. Hadrian decided to limit Rome's territorial expansion and to secure the limits established by Augustus Caesar. He visited nearly every Roman province and put affairs in order. A man of many abilities, Hadrian was a poet, a student of Greek culture, an architect, a builder, and a good soldier.

Wherever Hadrian traveled, he left monuments to himself, like Hadrian's Wall, built in northern England. During these travels, he made architectural drawings of buildings he wanted duplicated for his Italian retreat. Begun in 118, Hadrian's Villa was 20 years in the making; Hadrian died in 138, the year of its completion.

The villa was like a little town and could host 3,000 guests at a time, but after his death, no one was interested in maintaining the lavish complex. In 1450 Flavio Biondo mentioned the Villa of Hadrian as an interesting place to visit. No written notice of the villa had been made for 1,000 years. Pope Pius II said of it in 1461: "Time has ruined all; ivy covers the walls that once were clothed with tapestries and golden draperies; thorns and scrub flourish where once sat purple-clad tribunes and snakes infest the queen's chambers: such is the transient lot of human affairs." Tourists should include in their hurried schedules a half-day trip to the Villa of Hadrian near Tivoli.

Loving God, thank you for moral leaders. We pray that our national and
world leaders will be wise and compassionate in their actions.

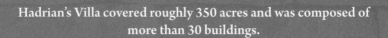

Hadrian's Villa covered roughly 350 acres and was composed of
more than 30 buildings.

Roman Baths

"And He said to him, 'Go, wash in the pool of Siloam' (which is translated, Sent). So he went and washed, and came back seeing."
John 9:7

During the empire, various public officials and emperors built large public baths for the pleasure and health of the citizens. Some of the grandest ruins in Rome are of the ancient public baths. Statues, fountains, large drains, and marble from the baths have been incorporated into many palaces and churches.

In 33 B.C. Agrippa, a public official whose duties included supervising the public baths, built the Baths of Agrippa near the Pantheon. Nero's Baths were built on Mars Field. Titus and Trajan built baths on the Aventine Hill and next to the Golden House of Nero, opposite the Colosseum. Septimius Severus built baths on the Palatine Hill. In 206 Caracalla built a 27-acre bathing complex south of the city to accommodate 3,000 bathers simultaneously.

In 298 Diocletian completed the Baths of Diocletian, begun by Maximian. This 32-acre hydraulic and artistic marvel could accommodate 1,600 bathers. Decorated with rare marble and gorgeous statues, these baths also included a semi-circular garden where the modern Piazza Esedra now features a large round fountain with naked maidens enjoying the constant spray of cool water. Ruins of the Baths of Diocletian are in front of Rome's modern train station. A fine museum is housed in part of the ruins.

Emperor Constantine built the last great imperial baths on the Quirinal Hill, near what is now the president's palace. In front of the palace, statues of the Horse Tamers, originally in the Baths of Constantine, salute visiting heads of state.

Several hours were required to go to the baths. At first it was prohibited to bathe before the eighth hour of the day. Women were required to bathe first, and then men were allowed to use the facilities. However, nude men and women could use the exercise room simultaneously.

Father, thank you for marvelous water. May we use it wisely.

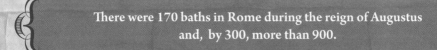

There were 170 baths in Rome during the reign of Augustus and, by 300, more than 900.

Diocletian

*"Yours, O LORD, is the greatness, The power and the glory, The victory and the majesty;
For all that is in heaven and in earth is Yours; Yours is the kingdom, O LORD, And You
are exalted as head over all."*
I Chronicles 29:11

Diocletian, one of the greatest administrators of the Roman Empire, is remembered for the evil he did in the service of religion. Born in the Roman province of Illyricum, what is now modern Albania and Croatia, in 245, he was proclaimed emperor by his troops in 284. His great concern was preserving the unity of the empire, which now stretched from Britain to Persia and included most of Europe and North Africa.

Diocletian thought one of the best ways to unite the empire was through religion. The first coins he had minted included the god Jupiter, and he zealously worshiped Mithras, whom many considered the guardian of the empire. On February 23, 303, the day of the god Terminus, an imperial edict ordered the destruction of churches and the confiscation of church properties, including cemeteries. Christian worship was forbidden. Clergy were imprisoned, tortured, and ordered to offer sacrifices to the ancient gods. Refusal to worship the gods resulted in death. Terror stalked the country. Persecutions were fierce and without pity. Historians consider this the last and worst persecution of Christianity in Rome.

In 311 the edict to persecute Christians was rescinded because it hadn't worked. Early Christian author Tertullian observed, "The blood of the martyrs had become the seed of the church." Many wonderful, faithful Christians had died for their faith.

Diocletian is also remembered for his baths, the largest of the public baths built in Rome. Later those same baths were made into the Church of St. Mary of the Angels, from designs by Michelangelo, something Diocletian could never have imagined.

*Loving Father, help us to live our lives in such a way
that we will leave a legacy of goodwill.*

**In 305, Diocletian resigned because of illness, becoming the first Roman
Emperor to voluntarily remove himself from office. He died in 316.**

Constantine the Great

"But God forbid that I should boast except in the cross of our Lord Jesus Christ."
Galatians 6:14a

Constantine was proclaimed emperor by his troops in England, when his father died in 306, and was the first Roman emperor to become a Christian. He was born about 275 to Constantius, emperor of the western provinces of Rome, and to Helen, a powerful Christian woman who influenced her son and the empire.

Emperor Diocletian had started a system of shared rule by two senior and two junior emperors. To establish himself as the one emperor, Constantine needed to conquer Maxentius in the capitol. In 312 he marched on Rome. The night before his army was to attack the city, he had a vision of a cross in the sky and decided to fight under the sign of the cross: *in hoc signo vince*, which means "in this sign, conquer." Constantine's forces defeated Maxentius at the Battle of the Milvian Bridge.

Constantine became a strong supporter of the growing Christian church. He did his best to conciliate both Christians and pagans. He ordered that a basilica be built on the Lateran property and that churches should be built over the tombs of St. Peter and St. Paul. In 321 he ordered that Sunday should become a public holiday, pleasing Christians and worshippers of Mithras and Apollo, the sun god. In 313 the Edict of Milan gave freedom of worship and equal legal rights to all religious groups. Constantine returned to Christians their confiscated property and deeded some public land to Christian groups for churches.

Before his death, Constantine was baptized. He is remembered for recognizing Christianity as a legal religion and for moving the center of empire to his new city of Constantinople.

Father, thank you for Christian leaders who look to you for guidance.

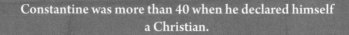

Constantine was more than 40 when he declared himself a Christian.

Battle of the Milvian Bridge

"I can do all things through Christ who strengthens me."
Philippians 3:13

When Constantine marched toward Rome, he had no siege equipment. The thick walls of Rome were adequate protection for Emperor Maxentius and his army. They remained securely inside. A spokesman for the Roman gods told Maxentius that on the 28th of October, "the enemy of Rome will die." The emperor interpreted the riddle as divine prophecy that he would be victorious and Constantine would be killed. He decided to leave the fortified city and engage in battle. To march north, the army needed to cross the Tiber River. Unfortunately, he had ordered the stone Milvian Bridge to be destroyed so the soldiers constructed a pontoon bridge.

Constantine, sure of God's protection, marched with his soldiers from Prima Porta toward Rome, the emblem of the cross on their shields. At Saxa Rubra the two armies first exchanged blows. Maxentius and his soldiers retreated toward Rome. The new pontoon bridge was not strong enough for the thundering hooves of the horses, and Emperor Maxentius and many of his soldiers fell into the Tiber River and drowned. Unopposed, Constantine marched into Rome and proclaimed himself Emperor. He was quick to give credit to God for his guidance and protection. Throughout Constantine's rule, he remembered how he won the battle for Rome.

The Battle of the Milvian Bridge was a turning point in the history of Europe. No longer were people forced to sacrifice to pagan gods. Through his *Edict of Toleration*, Constantine brought religious freedom to the Western world. One biographer, Hermann Doerries, wrote, "Only as a Christian could Constantine win the battle and only because the battle was won by a Christian Emperor did it become decisive for the destiny of the Roman Empire."

Gracious Father, help us to receive clearly and gladly your guidance to us.
Help us to win the victory over the evil that would destroy us.

**A reconstructed Milvian Bridge—*Ponte Milvio*—
stands at the same site today.**

Egyptians in Rome

"And [the Hebrews] built for Pharaoh supply cities, Pithom and Raamses."
Exodus 1:11b

Diplomats, Italian politicians, and American residents in Rome moved about the rooms of the American Consulate, talking about Rome and their current posts. The receptic was in honor of the assistant secretary of state and a Washington delegation. A young woma who had flown from Izmir had arrived early for some sightseeing. She had spent a morning in the Vatican Museum and was fascinated by the marvelous Egyptian Museum. Making conversation, she asked me, "How did all these Egyptian artifacts get to Italy?"

Egypt is one of the oldest civilizations in the world. Its influence on the ancient world is incalculable. Non-Egyptians were both intrigued with its mystery and afraid of its power. Ancient Egyptians called their land *Kam-t*. Canaanites knew it as *Misru*. Hebrews used the name in the dual form of *Mizraim* for Upper and Lower Egypt. From the moment (Egypt's ascendancy to power in the Mediterranean, a busy, healthy trade developed betweer Egypt and Rome. Romans were enamored with Egypt and the Egyptians.

Several Caesars brought many obelisks from Egypt in specially constructed ships that could stand the strain and weight of the heavy granite. The Egyptian temple of Isis, built in Mars Field in Rome during the empire, contained many Egyptian statues. The city's Egyptians lived near there. Emperor Hadrian was one of the most enthusiastic collectors of Egyptian art. Interested in architecture, he had architects accompany him on his journeys. T Villa of Hadrian contained many Egyptian sculptures that eventually came under the contro of the papacy and were put in the Vatican Museum.

In Baroque times, Egyptian sculptures, remaining from imperial days, were appropriated for varied uses. Beautiful lions and other statuary were incorporated into publi fountains and monuments in Piazza del Popolo, the Moses fountain by the Grand Hotel, St. Peter's Square, and other places. Egyptian obelisks and designs embellish Rome, as well as other capitol cities.

Father, as empires rise and fall, we are assured that your Kingdom is forever.

Egypt became a Roman province when Octavian defeated Marc Anthony in 30 B.C. at the Battle of Actium.

Fibonacci

"So teach us to number our days, That we may gain a heart of wisdom."
Psalm 90:12

XXV plus L is LXXV. For more than 1,000 years Romans did their math with these numerals. But as commerce increased and trade extended, it became difficult to compute large sums. Marco Polo brought the abacus from China about 1000. This tool was as revolutionary as the modern computer, but without simple numerals, zero, algebra, or geometry, it still was difficult to carry on international trade.

Fibonacci—a nickname given to Leonardo of Pisa posthumously—is credited with bringing into Europe the use of Arabic numerals, which introduced important algebraic concepts to Roman math. Fibonacci lived from about 1170 to 1240. While helping his father with business in North Africa, he learned about negative numbers, zero, and fractions. In the 13th century there was a renaissance in mathematics, science, and literature. Fibonacci's *The Book of the Abacus* explained these vital mathematical concepts.

Today Fibonacci is remembered for an equation he explained in the book through the example of rabbit reproduction. He posed a question: How many pairs of rabbits can be bred from one pair in one year? What's become known as the Fibonacci number is the answer. The number of rabbits grows exponentially as each new rabbit produces more animals to add to the original pair: $1 + 2 = 3$; $2 + 3 = 5$, $3 + 5 = 8$. And so on the sequence goes.

The Fibonacci numbers—which some mistakenly think he invented—are used today in more ways than can be described: scientists calculate population growth; stock brokers predict the market; architects study the increasing proportions to determine pleasing designs. Its principles are also found in nature—for example, pineapples and pinecones both have spirals winding clockwise and counterclockwise that are consecutive terms of the sequence—prompting some to call it God's Equation.

Father Creator, thank you for the mystery of mathematics in the construction of the universe, and for the tools of math that make our lives easier.

A statue of Fibonacci is in Pisa's cemetery.

The Knights of Malta

"They shall beat their swords into plowshares, And their spears into pruning hooks; Nation shall not lift up sword against nation, Neither shall they learn war anymore."
Isaiah 2:4b

Many tourists to Rome visit the Piazza of the Knights of Malta on the Aventine Hill to look through the keyhole of the doors to the Villa of the Knights of Malta. Through it is a perfect view of St. Peter's Basilica, framed by the arc of a long green arbor. It makes a great photograph when the camera is held steady against the small opening.

The Knights of Malta began in Amalfi around 1070 when they were dedicated to St. John the Baptist. During the Crusades the monastic community assumed military functions, protecting pilgrims and the sick. In 1113 they were recognized as a religious-military order and through donations from European monarchs and other wealthy Christians, the Knights obtained vast property throughout the Middle East and Europe. They fought in the Holy Land until the last Crusader fortress fell in 1291. They moved to Cyprus and in 1310 captured the island of Rhodes, from which they fought the Ottoman Turks in the Mediterranean. After fierce fighting, the Turks drove the Knights from Rhodes in 1522. In 1530 Charles V, the Holy Roman Emperor, ceded the island of Malta to the Knights, thus conferring on the Order the status of a sovereign state. They became known as the Knights of Malta. In 1798 the Knights lost Malta to Napoleon's troops, but they retain their title of Sovereign Order of the Knights of Malta, due to an accord with Malta. Since 1834, their official headquarters has been in Rome on Via Condotti near Via del Corso.

Across the piazza from the Knights' villa is a white wall, decorated with reliefs of obelisks, urns, masks, swords, shields, and other weapons of war. The suggestion of weapons, hung on a wall, gives tribute to the Knights' peaceful ministries of healing and caring for the poor.

Loving Father, may your children learn your ways of peace and harmony.

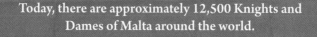

Today, there are approximately 12,500 Knights and
Dames of Malta around the world.

Plague

*"And that very hour He cured many of infirmities, afflictions, and evil spirits;
and to many blind He gave sight."*
Luke 7:21

Bubonic plague was probably brought to Europe from the Holy Land by Crusaders returning home. Between 1334 and 1351 the Black Death killed about one-fourth of Europe's population. The deadly plague attacked quickly. A person awoke in the morning, feeling fine. A small boil was often the first sign of illness; then the victim suffered chills and fever, headache and body pains. Lymph glands began to swell in the groin, armpits, and neck and sometimes became open sores. Often, before the day was ended, the patient was dead.

During the time of plague there were never enough hospitals or medical personnel to care for the ill and dying. With a high death rate, it was difficult to bury the diseased bodies. Infection spread quickly. During these times, selfless nuns and monks worked frantically to ease the suffering of the stricken, to minister to their families, and to assist orphaned children. Often the ministering nuns and monks contracted the disease themselves. Rarely did a person recuperate from the plague. Catherine of Sienna and other holy women ministered to the dying.

In 1576 a great plague struck again. Charles Borromeo, archbishop of Milan, worked to help the sick and the poor during that time of crisis. Fifty-three years later when the plague returned to Italy, it was called "the plague of St. Charles" for the canonized Borromeo who was remembered for his compassionate help with the dying.

La peste lo colga!—"Plague on it!"—is still a cry of exasperation, a curse on the hated source of trouble. By the 19th century, the plague was brought under control by the extermination of rats. Today Rome's cats are constantly on mouse duty, protecting people from disease-bearing rodents. Through current international agreements, nations report an outbreak of plague in any port.

***Great Physician, help us learn good health habits
to keep ourselves well and strong for your service.***

When the Black Death reached Italy in the 14th century, it swept
through the country in only three months.

Federigo, Duke of Urbino

"The rich man's wealth is his strong city."
Proverbs 10:15a

Born illegitimately, the death of the legitimate heir changed forever the fortunes of Federigo da Montefeltro, who ruled Urbino from 1444 to 1482. His influence is felt throughout this model city of the Renaissance.

Studying in Venice and Mantua, Federigo had a classical education and learned self-discipline and frugal living along with literature and the arts, sports, riding, swordsmanship, and a high sense of social obligation. As a *condottiere*, or a "paid warrior," he sold his skills to the highest bidder. He was remembered as a magnanimous victor, nearly always winning the battles in which he engaged. He was a man of his word, respected by friend and foe.

A portrait of the broken-nose Federigo, painted by Piero della Francesco, now hangs in the Uffizi Gallery in Florence. For 300 years the family of Federigo had governed no more than a few dozen square miles in the Apennines and remained relatively free from control by Venice, Milan, or the papal princes. After the assassination of his brother, Federigo consolidated several mountain fiefs and extended them into a state three times larger than his original inheritance. He ruled a territory about 60 miles by 60 miles, including 400 villages and 150,000 inhabitants. He maintained independence by playing off Rome against Venice or Florence against Rome.

Urbino was proud of the Duke who transformed her city into a model blend of nature and urbanity. The arts were encouraged, and buildings and streets provided a proper backdrop for social interaction. Five hundred people were in his court. The beautiful palace was furnished with exquisite furniture, paintings, sculpture, and musical instruments—many of which are now in museums in Florence, Milan, and in Windsor Castle. His library, the most complete in Europe, is now mostly in the Vatican Museum. The beautiful, well-planned city of Urbino stands as his finest monument.

Loving Lord, raise up capable, moral leaders
from our bright youth to lead our nation.

Missing an eye from a duel, Federigo preferred profiles painted of his good side instead of full-face portraits.

Machiavelli

"Let us walk properly, as in the day, not in revelry and drunkenness, not in lewdness and lust, not in strife and envy. But put on the Lord Jesus Christ, and make no provision for the flesh, to fulfill its lusts."
Romans 13:13-14

His name still stands for all that is suspicious and ruthless. Hundreds of references in the 17th century link his name with the Devil or the Evil One. He is considered the father of politics. Patterning much of what he wrote in *The Prince* on the ruthless tactics of Cesare Borgia, he asserted that a ruler must use any means, no matter how wicked, to eliminate his enemies and make his people obedient.

Born in Florence in 1469, Niccolò Machiavelli lived during the time when the Medici were driven from Florence and the Republic of Florence was founded. When the Medici returned to power in 1512, Machiavelli was arrested, tortured, and imprisoned. He was released on order of Pope Leo X. He spent the last 14 years of his life in retirement near Florence, writing poetry, comedies, and books on history and politics.

In his biographical novel *Then and Now*, W. Somerset Maugham has Machiavelli describe his motivations to a servant:

"Take care that like me you do not get a reputation for riot, since if you do no one will think you sensible, but notice men's moods and adapt yourself to them; laugh with them when they are merry and pull a long face when they are solemn. It is absurd to be wise with fools and foolish with the wise: you must speak to each one in his own language. Be courteous; it costs little and helps much; to be of use and to know how to show yourself of use is to be doubly useful; it is idle to please yourself if you do not please others, and remember that you please them more by ministering to their vices than by encouraging their virtues."

He sounds like some modern politicians!

God of truth and wisdom, help our political leaders to lead honestly.

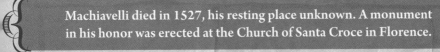

Machiavelli died in 1527, his resting place unknown. A monument in his honor was erected at the Church of Santa Croce in Florence.

Christopher Columbus

"His dominion shall be 'from sea to sea, And from the River to the ends of the earth.'"
Zechariah 9:10b

Genoa native Christopher Columbus had an overwhelming desire to sail east by going west to find a new trade route to China. Born in 1451, Christopher Columbus was named for St. Christopher, patron saint of travelers. As he matured, he determined it was his destiny to carry the divine word of Christ across the mighty ocean; *Cristoforo Colombo* means "the Christ-bearing dove."

Living in a busy port city on the Tyrrhenian Sea, it is probable the red-haired Columbus had heard tales of many interesting voyages and had possibly been a crewmember on various ships by his 20th birthday. Genoa had a noted school of mapmakers where Columbus probably learned the basics of mapmaking. Later he and his brother had a mapmaking business in Lisbon, Portugal.

Though Columbus left Genoa when he was about 22, he always referred to himself as *Genovese*—a person from Genoa—and not as Italian, for Genoa did not become a part of Italy until the 19th century. It took years for Columbus to find a sponsor for his fantastic dream, but he somehow convinced the king and queen of Spain to underwrite his exploration into unknown waters. With three ships, the Nina, the Pinta, and the Santa Maria, Columbus set sail from Palos, Spain, on August 3, 1492. He was 41.

Sailing first by the Canary Islands, and then on the great ocean that was thought to lie between Europe and Asia, they sailed west for 33 days. The sailors had become discouraged and wanted to return to Spain. Columbus promised them that if they did not see land within three days, they would return to Europe. The first land sighted in the Western Hemisphere by Columbus was the eastern coast of San Salvador, an island in the Bahamas. On October 12, the Spaniards finally entered a shallow bay. Greeted by naked natives, the Spanish planted the royal standard of Spain, claiming the land in the name of Spain and of God.

Bless us Lord. Give us strength and stamina to accomplish your purposes.

Christopher Columbus reached the American mainland on his third voyage in 1498.

Galileo Galilei

"And you shall know the truth, and the truth shall make you free."
John 8:32

Galileo Galilei lived at the same time as many Renaissance geniuses who were encouraged by Florence's wealthy Medici family to discover new ways of learning. Born in Pisa in 1564, Galileo spent his childhood in Pisa and Florence. His father was a musician and taught his son to play the lute. His parents made him responsible for helping support the family. Even when he was an old man, he supported his siblings.

As a child he enjoyed mathematical games. His experiments challenged long-accepted theories, such as the idea that the earth is flat and the sun moves around the earth. Galileo entered the University of Pisa as a medical student, but the lure of mathematics was too great. He was entranced with geometry and the teachings of Euclid.

Galileo invented the sector, a type of compass still used by draftsmen. Through the experiments of a Dutch scientist, Galileo was inspired to develop a telescope. Skeptical Venetian leaders refused to look through the telescope, thinking it was a trick. Sea captains, generals, and kings bought them to gain advantage by seeing ships and armies miles away. Galileo set up a telescope factory and ordering service in his villa; income from this business gave him funds for experiments. He constructed a large telescope and viewed the heavens. He was astonished to see that the moon was not a smooth orb but had a surface marked by mountains and valleys. In 1610 he discovered four of Jupiter's moons and named them for the Medici family. He recognized Saturn's true form but did not discover its rings. He looked at the sun through smoked lenses, but the bright light eventually blinded him. His brilliance and enlightened mind changed the science of his day.

Loving Father, thank you for determined people who relentlessly search for truth. Thank you for the Christ, the way, the truth, and the life.

From the top of Pisa's bell tower, Galileo threw lightweight and heavy objects to prove they fell at the same rate of speed.

Giuseppe Garibaldi

"So the women sang as they danced, and said: 'Saul has slain his thousands,
And David his ten thousands.'"
I Samuel 18:7

His name was known around the world. Streets and public squares were named for him in towns from Italy to Uruguay. Stores in Manchester and Milan, Boston and Bologna, London and Livorno sold statuettes, busts, medallions, and china figurines of the bearded hero. Wherever he went after his stunning victories, Giuseppe Garibaldi was lauded, treated like a liberating hero.

Garibaldi was a Sardinian peasant-general who fought to unite a fragmented Italy. His aims were to get the Austrians out of northern Italy, to wrest from the pope his temporal power in central Italy, and to remove the Bourbon king from the Kingdom of the Two Sicilies in the south. After taking part in an unsuccessful rebellion against the king of Sardinia in 1834, Garibaldi went to South America and fought with other countries for their independence. In 1848 Garibaldi returned to help defend Italy against the French. He then went to New York City and experienced democracy, which he wanted for Italy.

Returning home and fired with passion for uniting Italy, Garibaldi and a poorly equipped force set sail from Sardinia for Sicily. He led about 1,000 men, astonishing Europe when his forces quickly captured the main port city of Palermo. With open arms, Sicily and southern Italy welcomed the liberator. Garibaldi entered Naples without firing a shot. Driving out the Bourbon army, he marched north.

Garibaldi resigned his command to King Victor Emmanuel II at Teano. Though he wanted Italy to have a democracy, he knew that a kingdom with a strong ruler would be the best solution to unify a long-fragmented peninsula and several islands, and both men agreed that it was best that the French and Austrians were out of the country.

Years later, after Mussolini's fall, Italy was able to have a democracy with elected representation. Garibaldi's dream finally came true.

Father, thank you for liberty, and for those who protect our freedoms.

Garibaldi's soldiers were called "red shirts," for showing their disdain for blood by wearing bright red.

Count Cavour

"The LORD has broken the staff of the wicked, The scepter of the rulers."
Isaiah 14:5

Count Camillo Benso di Cavour, a Machiavellian-type statesman, is honored in Italy for his efforts to put fragmented Italy back together again. Born in 1810 of a noble family in Turin, he served from 1852 to 1859 and from 1860 to 1861 as Sardinia's Prime Minister. The Kingdom of Sardinia was ruled by Victor Emmanuel II of the House of Savoy. In 1859, Sardinia and France fought a war against Austria, which also ruled Lombardy. After Sardinia defeated the Austrians, Sardinia annexed Lombardy and all the states of central Italy except the papal states near Rome.

He had a reputation for keeping his strategies hidden. Once when he needed to plot with a revolutionary, Cavour said, "Come to see me whenever you like, but come at daybreak, and let no one else see or know. If I am questioned in Parliament or by diplomats, I shall deny you, like Peter, and say, 'I know him not.'"

His undying hatred for Giuseppe Garibaldi may have proved fatal. Cavour described him as "a man so heroic of stature in one field, so dwarflike in others," a man "whom someone described as having the heart of a child and the head of a buffalo." Their contempt for each other was mutual. Garibaldi so despised Cavour that the general vowed to cut off his own hand rather than allow Cavour to shake it. At times when Garibaldi, a member of the newly formed Parliament, had to speak to Cavour, he carefully kept his hands under his cloak. After a bitter quarrel and debate in Parliament, Cavour said, "If emotion could have killed, I should have died during that hour." Cavour never recovered from the complete emotional exhaustion of the verbal battle of that day. Within a year, his health declined rapidly, and he died on June 2, 1861.

Loving Father, help us love and appreciate our co-workers.

Tourists to Turin should visit the birthplace
of the count, the Palazzo Cavour.

Mussolini

"Like a roaring lion and a charging bear Is a wicked ruler over poor people."
Proverbs 28:15

During Benito Mussolini's prime, his name was linked with Adolph Hitler's as Italy joined Germany and Japan to form the Axis powers during World War II. For more than two decades, Mussolini—*Il Duce* or "the leader"—was Italy's Prime Minister, then Dictator. Today his name is seen in only one prominent place in Rome: on a marble obelisk at Piazza d' Italia near the Tiber River.

Born in 1883 to a blacksmith father and schoolteacher mother, Mussolini became editor of *Avanti*, the leading socialist newspaper in Italy, in 1912. He managed through a series of events to become head of the Fascist party, which he had founded in Milan in 1919. By October 1922, the Fascists were powerful enough to force the weak King Victor Emmanuel III to ask Mussolini to be the premier of the government. The new prime minister declared a war of aggression against Ethiopia, promising to extend the boundaries of a new Italian Empire. Drunk with power, Mussolini joined forces with Hitler, who had flattered Mussolini into thinking victory and fame were within his grasp.

Heartache and disgrace were Italy's rewards for engaging in World War II. While the German army was well-fed, Italians and their army had scant fare. Survivors of the war say that cats and dogs disappeared from city streets. After the Allied invasion, Mussolini and his council came to an impasse. Afraid for their lives, Mussolini and his mistress fled from Rome in a car. On April 28, 1945, at Lake Como, underground forces stopped their car and killed them. Their bodies were taken to Milan where they were hung by the heels in a downtown piazza.

Today some remember Il Duce as a leader who made the trains run on time, created employment for the needy, and encouraged the arts. Others remember that he led Italy in a disgraceful, costly war that left the country poor and defeated.

***Almighty God, we pray for leaders who humble themselves
to lead with Christian principles.***

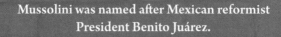

**Mussolini was named after Mexican reformist
President Benito Juárez.**

Liberation of Rome

"Stand fast therefore in the liberty by which Christ has made us free, and do not be entangled again with a yoke of bondage."
Galatians 5:1

In October 1942 British General Bernard Montgomery pushed Italo-German armies into Tunisia. By November a large force of British and American troops under the direction of American General Dwight D. Eisenhower landed on beaches of Morocco and Algeria where 950,000 Italian and German soldiers died. In May 1943 the Axis army in Tunisia surrendered. Franklin Roosevelt and Winston Churchill met in Casablanca to plan the invasion of Europe.

Secure in North Africa, the Allies were positioned to invade Sicily. Sicilians deserted their military posts, deciding they had rather live for family and Italy instead of die for Mussolini and Hitler. From Sicily Allied troops landed at Reggio Calabria on the toe of Italy, and at Salerno, Nettuno, and Anzio. Landings were costly. Many Allied and Axis soldiers are buried in vast cemeteries at those strategic sites. Churchill wanted Allied troops to focus on a quick invasion of Italy and push toward Rome, but General Eisenhower invaded southern France on the Riviera, and Allied soldiers fighting in Italy were deprived of reinforcements.

Allied troops fought northward toward Rome with slow and torturous advance. For months the Allies tried to dislodge the Germans north of Naples at Monte Cassino, a historic Benedictine monastery that the Allies finally destroyed. Mussolini's pact with Hitler had pauperized Italy; survivors in Italy say they happily cheered the liberating Allied troops when they marched into Rome on June 4. Pope Pius XII had implored both powers to spare Rome and its treasures from destruction. His request was honored.

The Allies required the Italians to decide the type of government they would have. After liberation, Italians voted to reject the monarchy and establish a democracy with a president, prime minister, and a legislature of house and senate. Italians are still learning what democracy means. Political leaders have formed a different government nearly every year since they voted to establish democratic government.

Lord, you have given us life and the concept of liberty.
Help us learn to respect and cooperate with others.

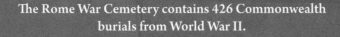

The Rome War Cemetery contains 426 Commonwealth burials from World War II.

The May King

"But when his heart was lifted up, and his spirit was hardened in pride, he was deposed from his kingly throne, and they took his glory from him"
Daniel 5:20

King Umberto II ruled Italy for a month after World War II. His father, King Victor Emmanuel III, had condoned the leadership of Benito Mussolini, but because of his association with fascism, the Italians wanted a change after the war. In an effort to save the monarchy, Victor Emmanuel III resigned in favor of his son, but it was too late.

The fourth king of modern Italy, Umberto II had little time to enjoy his position. In June 1946 Italians voted for their nation to be a democracy, and Umberto—the May King—and his family were exiled to Portugal.

Suffering from cancer, in 1983 Umberto asked to be allowed to return to Italy to die, which the government denied, even refusing him the privilege of being buried in Italy. Umberto died March 18, 1983, 37 years after he left Rome. Through the years, many kings, dukes, and counts of the House of Savoy were interred in the ancient Abbey of Hautecombe in France, near Geneva, Switzerland. It was this place that was chosen for Umberto.

Italians were very interested in who would inherit the family treasures. For centuries the House of Savoy had owned the Sacro Sindone, the Holy Shroud that was supposed to have been wrapped around the crucified body of Christ. Umberto willed the relic to the papacy. It is kept in a church in Turin, which had been the capital of Savoy. Umberto had inherited his father's splendid coin collection containing many medals and items of military interest. These he willed to the Italian people. A street in Rome is named for him. Other streets, monuments, a women's hospital, and the American Embassy building are named in honor of members of the House of Savoy. A simple pizza with red tomato sauce, fresh green basil, and white mozzarella cheese honors Queen Margherita, an enduring honor for the mother of the May King.

King of kings and Lord of lords, we bow before you in your majesty and glory.

Umberto served as King of Italy for 33 days, from May 9 to June 12, 1946.

Swiss Guards

*"Be strong and of good courage; do not be afraid, nor be dismayed,
for the LORD your God is with you wherever you go."*
Joshua 1:9b

Five hundred years ago when European nations were constantly at war, Swiss soldiers hired themselves out as mercenaries for various countries. During the struggle to maintain his papacy, Pope Julius II hired Swiss troops to get the French out of his homeland near Genoa. Julius then continued to employ the loyal, skilled Swiss soldiers. Two decades later, on May 6, 1527, Pope Clement VII and the Vatican were besieged by the troops of Charles V, King of Spain and the Holy Roman Empire. One hundred forty-seven Swiss soldiers died that day. Forty-two surviving guards, the Pope, and others were besieged in the fortress of Castel Sant' Angelo for seven months.

After the Pope's temporal powers ceased, it was no longer necessary for the Pope to have an army, but wherever the Pope goes these bodyguards bear final responsibility for his safety. They are the world's oldest, active military force. Guards are recruited in several Catholic cantons of Switzerland. They must be under 30 years old, at least 1.74 meters tall (5 feet 9 inches), and in good health. They are of good reputation, unmarried, and have completed basic military service in Switzerland. Salaries are low, hours are long, their training is arduous.

Their colorful costumes, worn on special occasions, were redesigned in 1919. The original design is sometimes attributed to Michelangelo or to Raphael. The everyday working costume is dark-blue shirt and pants with a beret. Guards standing on duty hold a halberd, a very long spear with a battleaxe on the end. Modern bodyguards who accompany the Pope dress in dark blue business suits and blend in with the crowds. The Guards are committed to protecting the Pope, who likes to be close to the people, despite dangers of terrorist attacks. A swearing-in ceremony for newly inducted Guards is held in St. Peter's every May 6.

Lord, protect us from evil.

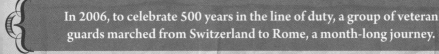

In 2006, to celebrate 500 years in the line of duty, a group of veteran guards marched from Switzerland to Rome, a month-long journey.

Section III
Artistic Italy

Virgil

"To give light to those who sit in darkness and the shadow of death,
To guide our feet into the way of peace."
Luke 1:79

Considered by many as the greatest of Latin poets, Virgil lived from 70 to 19 B.C. He was born in a village near Mantua in northern Italy to a farmer. He was educated in Cremona, Milan, Naples, and Rome, studying philosophy and rhetoric. Maecenas, a wealthy assistant to Emperor Augustus, liked his writings and became his patron. *The Georgics*, a poem in four books on the life of the farmer and a celebration of Italy and agriculture, established Virgil as the foremost poet of the early empire.

The last 10 years of his life he devoted to writing *The Aeneid*, a mythological epic in 12 books that revealed the noble, Greek beginnings of the Romans. He described the seven-year wanderings of Aeneas, who escaped from Troy as it burned at the end of the Trojan War. Fleeing from the burning city, Aeneas carried his aged father on his shoulders and led his young son by the hand. (Bernini's statue of this is in the Borghese Museum in Rome.) Aeneas assembled a fleet of ships and sailed the eastern Mediterranean Sea with the surviving Trojans. He and his crew were shipwrecked on the coast of what is now Libya where Queen Dido of Carthage fell in love with Aeneas. She committed suicide when he left for Italy. After landing at the mouth of the Tiber River in Italy, Aeneas fought King Turnus of Latium and won the hand of Princess Lavinia. His son was founder of Alba Longa, mother city of Rome.

In 19 B.C. Virgil went to Greece, hoping to revise *The Aeneid* on his journey. He met Augustus in Athens and returned with him home. Virgil became ill and died shortly after their arrival in southern Italy. On his deathbed he gave instructions that *The Aeneid* should be destroyed, but Augustus ordered two poets to finish it, and it was published after Virgil's death.

Dear Lord, lead and guide us in the activities of our busy lives.

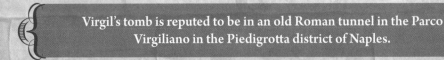

Virgil's tomb is reputed to be in an old Roman tunnel in the Parco Virgiliano in the Piedigrotta district of Naples.

Cimabue and Giotto

"And the LORD God formed man of the dust of the ground, and breathed into his nostrils the breath of life; and man became a living being."
Genesis 2:7

About 1240 Bencivieni di Pepo, or Cimabue, was born in Florence. As a young man he liked to watch immigrant Byzantine artists working in Florence. Cimabue broke with the traditions of popular Byzantine painting and began to paint people and things as he saw them. He painted pictures and frescoes and made mosaics for many churches in Tuscany and Umbria. Legend has it that once when Cimabue was traveling through the countryside, he saw a young boy tending his family's sheep. With a lump of charcoal the boy sketched the picture of a sheep on a large rock. The likeness of the sheep was so remarkable that Cimabue arranged with the boy's father for his son, Giotto, to live and study with him.

That boy, Giotto di Bondone, was born about 1267 near Florence. After serving an apprenticeship under Cimabue, he worked in Assisi, Pisa, Arezzo, Rimini, Rome, and Naples. Giotto's method of presenting human figures in life-like, rounded sculptural forms was a new way of painting. Gone were rigid medieval stylization and rules. He emphasized the human and real instead of the divine and the ideal, which was revolutionary in an age dominated by religion. Once when the pope sent an emissary to collect samples from several artists, it was reported, "Giotto ... took a sheet of paper and a brush dipped in red, closed his arm to his side, so as to make a sort of compass of it, and then with a twist of his hand drew such a perfect circle that it was a marvel to see." It was more than enough to demonstrate his skill.

His most famous frescoes are of the life of St. Francis, painted in Assisi's Upper Church in the Basilica of St. Francis in Assisi. Giotto died in Florence in 1337 and is buried in the Church of Santa Croce.

Maker of heaven and earth, thank you for creating our beautiful world.

Best known for his frescoes, Giotto was architect for Florence's bell tower, which stands 288-feet high.

Dante Alighieri

"Now I saw a new heaven and a new earth, for the first heaven and the first earth had passed away. Also there was no more sea."
Revelation 21:1

Dante Alighieri was born in Florence in 1265 into a family of lower nobility. When he was about 9 years old, he met Beatrice Portinari, who embodied all he could imagine in a perfect, lovely lady. He saw her again nine years later. Promised in marriage to someone else, he loved Beatrice in an abstract way and was inspired to artistic greatness by thoughts of her.

Active in the political life of Florence and involved with the Guelph Party, Dante was banned from the city for a period of two years. A heavy fine was levied with the stipulation that if he failed to pay, he would be condemned to death if he ever returned to Florence. In exile, he lived in Verona and other northern Italian cities, in Paris, and eventually in Ravenna.

His first important literary work was *La Vita Nuova*, a collection of sonnets and songs with a prose commentary. Reflecting the love poetry of French troubadours, it concerned his idealized love of Beatrice and was written in the Tuscan dialect. It is considered one of the greatest verse sequences in European literature.

The Divine Comedy, his epic masterpiece, is an allegorical narrative. Writing with strong poetic rhythms and patterns, he tells of his imaginary journey through hell, purgatory, and heaven. In each of these three places, Dante meets mythological, historical, and contemporary people. In the afterlife these people receive the rewards or punishments of their life on earth. Each character symbolizes a human virtue or fault. The reward or punishment gives meaning to their choices and actions in the universal scheme. The Latin writer Virgil guides him through hell and purgatory, and then Beatrice guides Dante through paradise. This long work provides a summary of political, scientific, philosophical, and religious thought of the time, and for centuries has been studied, memorized, and quoted by students and scholars throughout the world.

We are grateful, Father, for brilliant thinkers who dare to share their thoughts with others.

Dante died in September 1321, in Ravenna, and is buried there.

Brunelleschi's Dome

"The voice of the LORD makes the deer give birth, And strips the forests bare;
And in His temple everyone says, 'Glory!'"
Psalm 29:9

Every European city is characterized by its central place of worship. In 1296 the foundation stone was laid for the new cathedral of Florence, the dome of which still dominates the city's horizon.

About 1330, The Wool Merchants Guild—Florence's largest, wealthiest, most powerful guild—began administering the work of the duomo. Unfortunately, the Black Death came to Italy and shrank the population by four-fifths in 1347. Workers were imported from eastern Europe to ease labor shortages. By 1355 only the façade and walls of the nave had been built. The nave's vault was finished in 1366. Having no complete plans, the architect next considered how to build the dome. Any modern contractor would have complete architectural drawings and a guaranteed date of completion before beginning construction. But this was the Middle Ages: one thing at a time.

The Wool Merchants sponsored a contest to find the best architect-engineer to design and complete the building's dome. The winner was Filippo Brunelleschi, a Florentine artist who had worked for 20 years in Rome where he studied ancient architecture, especially the Pantheon. A short, ugly, brash bachelor, Brunelleschi had his supporters and his enemies. For more than 20 years he devised machinery to lift heavy loads of marble, sandstone, and bricks to workmen on narrow ledges. Each day Brunelleschi climbed the equivalent of 40 stories to supervise the workmen.

As the dome progressed, Brunelleschi solved each problem as it arose. He learned how to make the dome smaller and smaller at the top without it falling in on itself and how to use various types of stones and marble to construct different parts. Throughout the building project, it was necessary to deal with jealous artists, problems of supply, and wars. He died April 15, 1446, and was eventually buried in the church where "Brunelleschi's Dome" is his greatest monument.

Father, may our lives be blessed as we worship in your holy places.

St. Peter's in Rome, St. Paul's in London, and the U.S. Capitol in Washington, D.C., were all built with techniques and designs by Brunelleschi.

Florence and Her Artisans

"And as for Zillah, she also bore Tubal-Cain,
an instructor of every craftsman in bronze and iron."
Genesis 4:22a

Florence's modern artists and artisans can make most anything you need. It's amazing to see the variety of their craftsmanship. Tourists and Florentines watch artisans create fine hand-tooled leather bags and shoes, jewelry, pottery, woodcarvings, and wrought-iron objects.

Florence's oldest artifacts date back to Etruscan times. The city survived barbarian invasions, wars, and plagues and, by the 12th century, had developed a republican government. But political allegiance was divided. The strongest party in medieval Florence was the Guelphs, those faithful to the Pope; although the Ghibellines, who were faithful to the Holy Roman Emperor, were also numerous. Artisans then made weapons, armor, and uniforms.

In the 16th century Cosimo I Medici became Grand Duke of Tuscany. For 200 years the Medici dynasty ruled Florence, depriving Tuscany of her liberty, but giving her economic prosperity and artistic and scientific prestige. The Medici family is still best known for its patronage of the arts; some of Florence's most well-known artists worked during this period of the Italian Renaissance.

Throughout her history, Florence has been a city of creative people. Her greatest challenges came during World War II when Florentines destroyed some of her own bridges over the Arno River to make it difficult for the German occupation forces to function well. But both Axis and Allied powers refrained from destroying this historic city. However, nature has sometimes done what warring armies refused. Through the years plagues have killed thousands. Several floods have washed through Florence's streets, destroying art and human beings, including the devastating flood on November 4, 1966. Whatever the challenges of the times, Florence's creative people continue to host millions of tourists who come each year to enjoy the rich artistic treasures of past and present.

Father, thank you for the arts that enhance our lives
through the beauty of sight, sound, and touch.

Today there are more than 60 art museums
and galleries in Florence.

Ghiberti's Doors of Paradise

"Lift up your heads, O you gates! And be lifted up, you everlasting doors!
And the King of glory shall come in."
Psalm 24:7

St. John the Baptist, patron saint of Florence, was honored in the 11th century with the building of an octagonal church. When the construction of the cathedral was begun across the street in 1296, St. John's Church became known as the Baptistery. In 1336 Andrea Pisano completed a set of bronze doors that were installed at the main entrance to the Baptistery. In 1403 Lorenzo Ghiberti—a sculptor and goldsmith—won a contest to design a second set of bronze doors. Ghiberti and his studio worked 21 years on the doors, which weigh 34,000 pounds.

Ghiberti's skill and flawless work enhanced the reputation of Florence as an important city. In 1425 he was commissioned to design and make another set of doors for the Baptistery. These doors have 10 large panels with scenes from the Old Testament. Another 20 years was necessary to complete the work. Working in bronze requires great skill, strength, and time. In order to make the doors and deliver them to the place where they were installed, the workshop needed to be as close to the Baptistery as possible. A workshop with a large furnace was set up across the street. The doors are in harmony with the rest of the gothic building. Its architecture, mosaics, and statues are testimony to centuries of dedicated work and love for the church. Crowds of people constantly gather in front of the doors. They look at the scenes, executed in high and low relief, the masterpiece of an incredible artist of matchless skill and a testimony to his faith in God.

During the devastating 1966 flood of the Arno River, many Florentine art treasures were damaged beyond repair. Among the damaged treasures were the doors to the Baptistery. Heavy wrought-iron gates, through which the doors can be seen, now protect the unique, restored doors, important to Florentines and to art lovers everywhere.

Loving father, as your children, we anticipate entering
the real gates of Paradise and being with you eternally.

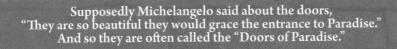

Supposedly Michelangelo said about the doors,
"They are so beautiful they would grace the entrance to Paradise."
And so they are often called the "Doors of Paradise."

Leonardo da Vinci

Leonardo da Vinci is thought by many to be the epitome of a "Renaissance Man." A painter, sculptor, architect, engineer, scientist, and musician, his notebooks—written in mirror writing—still amaze the scientific world with his vision. He was born to a wealthy Tuscan notary and a peasant woman in the town of Vinci near Florence. He spent his childhood learning from books and from observation in Tuscany's hills and valleys. When the family moved to Florence, fine teachers shaped his life, assuring a brilliant intellectual and artistic career. Apprenticed to Andrea del Verrocchio when he was 12, it was apparent to everyone that the student had surpassed the master when Leonardo painted a kneeling angel in Verrocchio's *Baptism of Christ*. Leonardo began to receive large commissions for his own works. His *Ginevra de' Benci* from this period is now in the National Gallery in Washington, D.C.

Around 1482 Leonardo went to work for the duke of Milan, Ludovico Sforza. While there he painted *The Last Supper* on the wall of the refectory in the Monastery of Santa Maria delle Grazie.

Leonardo then entered the service of Cesare Borgia, duke of Romagna and son of Pope Alexander VI, as the duke's architect and engineer. He returned to Florence and began painting the *Mona Lisa*, for which he seemed to have a special affection and which now hangs in the Louvre in Paris. In 1507 he became court painter to King Louis XII of France, who was living in Milan. In 1514 he moved to Rome where he did scientific experiments under the patronage of Pope Leo X. He then worked in France in the service of King Francis I. He lived his last years at the Chateau de Clous, near Amboise in France, where he died. More than 500 years later, the works of Leonardo da Vinci are still among the most recognized in the world.

Father, thank you for gifted people whose discoveries and artistic creations encourage others.

While in Milan, Leonard da Vinci wrote *Treatise on Painting*, one of the first books on how to paint.

Michelangelo, Sculptor

"Commit your works to the LORD, And your thoughts will be established."
Proverbs 16:3

Michelangelo Buonarroti was born in 1475 near Florence. His wet nurse was the wife of a stonecutter, and he often joked that he had grown up with marble dust in his mouth. He seemed destined to be an artist. His father, a Florentine official, placed his 13-year-old son in the workshop of Domenico Ghirlandaio, one of the best painters in Florence. Soon after, he began studying at the sculpture school in the Medici gardens. The wealthy and powerful Lorenzo de Medici invited the boy to live in his palace and eat at the table with artists, poets, humanists, and other visitors. After Lorenzo's death, Michelangelo worked in Bologna and then in Rome. He was fascinated with newly excavated ruins and classical statues. He said he was a "pupil of The Torso," the remnant of an ancient statue of a rugged athlete, now displayed in the Vatican Museum.

His first large-scale sculpture was of a young Bacchus, now housed in Florence's Bargello Museum. One of his most famous works of art is his first *Pietà*, which he finished while in Rome when he was 24 years old. A calm, grieving Mary holds her dead son on her lap. After Michelangelo overheard some tourists suggesting that a Milanese sculptor might have sculpted it, he climbed through a window into St. Peter's Basilica at night and carved a ribbon over the Madonna's breast with the words, "Michelangelo Buonarroti made this." This is the only piece he ever signed. His statues of Moses, Leah, and Rachel are in Rome's Church of St. Peter-in-Chains.

In Piazza Michelangelo on a hill above Florence, there is a bronze copy of his larger-than-life David—the original of which is in the Academia—and a breath-taking view of the city and the Arno River.

We are grateful, creative Lord, for the spark of creativity in the human spirit.

When the David was carefully cleaned in 2004, preparing it for a 500-years celebration, it was calculated that the ankles support six tons of marble.

Michelangelo's Moses

*"But since then there has not arisen in Israel a prophet like Moses,
whom the LORD knew face to face."*
Deuteronomy 34:10

Pope Julius II, a vain warrior pope, wanted to build an adequate tomb for himself over St. Peter's tomb in the Basilica of St. Peter. Julius persuaded Michelangelo to undertake the design and sculptures of the large, elaborate tomb. Michelangelo spent eight arduous months in the mountains above Carrara looking for exactly the right marble for the statues. He selected 110 tons of flawless white marble. After Michelangelo set up his workshop in Rome, Julius refused to pay for the marble and its costly transport. Michelangelo fled to Florence, and the pope was forced to beg him to return to Rome.

Because of wars, fickleness, and refusal to pay expenses, the work on the tomb was delayed time and again in favor of other projects. Michelangelo referred to the unfinished project as "the tragedy of the tomb." He worked under seven different popes, all the while being plagued by the heirs of Julius to finish the tomb. Eventually completed when the sculptor was an old man, the tomb was placed in the monastery church of St. Peter-in-Chains, across the river from St. Peter's Basilica. Moses, the Hebrew lawgiver, is the dominating figure of the tomb.

While Moses was on Mount Sinai with God, the Hebrews worshipped the golden calf, an idol they had made. In the statue, the stone tablets of the Law of God are in Moses' hands; he is angry to see the Hebrews' idolatry. The statue of the seated Moses captures the moment before he threw down the stone tablets, breaking them.

Many stories are told about *Moses*. It is said that when Michelangelo finished it, he was so impressed with its life-like quality that he ordered it, "Speak!" When the statue didn't obey, he struck the right knee with his mallet, and a small chip marred the perfect statue. Others say he deliberately chipped the knee so the statue wouldn't be perfect.

*Creator God, thank you for laws that give boundaries
and directions to our lives.*

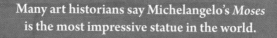

**Many art historians say Michelangelo's *Moses*
is the most impressive statue in the world.**

Raphael Sanzio

"And let the beauty of the LORD our God be upon us,
And establish the work of our hands for us; Yes, establish the work of our hands."
Psalm 90:17

Born in Urbino in 1483, Raphael Sanzio received training from his painter-father, Giovanni Santi, whose studio is now a museum. Raphael's messy pallet lies on his work table. The delicate miniature pieces he painted in his youth are displayed in Paris' Louvre and in the National Gallery, London. When he was 16, Raphael went to Perugia, capital of Umbria, to study with Perugino. There he mastered techniques of light, color, graceful figures, landscape settings, and design; this is known as his Umbrian period. His Florentine period began in 1504. He learned from Masaccio how to group figures and paint draperies. From Fra Bartolommeo he learned the secrets of modeling and expressing spiritual beauty. From Leonardo da Vinci he learned how to paint gracefully; and from Michelangelo, the importance of anatomy in portraying the human body convincingly.

His Roman period began in 1508 when Pope Julius II commissioned him to design and paint frescoes in four small rooms in the Vatican Palace. The most famous of these is *The School of Athens*. In an open architectural space, which modeled what the new St. Peter's might look like, Plato, Aristotle, and other ancient philosophers walk and discuss the meaning of life. Portraits of Michelangelo, Leonardo da Vinci, Masaccio, and Raphael himself represent famous Athenians.

His 12 years in Rome were busy. In 1514 Pope Leo X appointed him chief architect of St. Peter's Basilica and director of all excavations of antiquities in and near Rome. Raphael died in Rome on his 37th birthday, April 6, 1520. He was buried with great honor in the Pantheon, a place of worship, where Romans have honored pagan gods, kings of the united Italy, and Mary, the mother of Jesus. Tourists and art lovers bring flowers to his tomb and honor the artistic genius whose paintings were so exquisite that he has been called the Divine Raphael.

Divine Creator, help us develop the creative talents you give us.

Raphael's *The Transfiguration*, now in the Vatican Museum and considered his greatest work, was finished after his death by Giulio Romano, a pupil.

Palladio, Prince of Architects

"Unless the LORD builds the house, They labor in vain who build it."
Psalm 127:1a

Italy enjoyed a surge of building and expansion during the 16th century when architecture, painting, and sculpture achieved the status of fine arts. High Renaissance artists produced works that are still the ultimate examples of good workmanship. One of the best architects, Andrea di Pietro della Gondola, was born in Padua in 1524. Assistant to two stone carvers in Vicenza near Venice, Andrea also worked on an addition to a villa outside Vicenza. The villa's owner, Italian humanist Giangiorgio Trissino, called him Palladio, a play on the name of Pallas Athena, Greek goddess of wisdom.

Trissino sent Palladio to Rome to study the architecture of the Pantheon and other buildings. The stonecutter decided to be an architect. Palladio's major buildings are villas, palaces, and churches, mostly in or near Vicenza and Venice. One of Palladio's most famous buildings, Villa Rotonda, resembles a Greek Temple with four porches, one on each side. Palladio wrote *Four Books of Architecture* in 1570. This enduring work was translated in English in 1738 and was of tremendous influence on Thomas Jefferson. Drawings and architectural suggestions from the book no doubt influenced the buildings of Washington, D.C., the University of Virginia, and many state capitols.

Palladio designed and constructed many villas for wealthy families as investments and summer homes. The villas were rather like aristocratic farms, similar to American plantations. Palladio designed an imposing central building with wings and with secondary service buildings. Only 19 of the villas remain, some now functioning as museums. Venice has two Palladian churches. San Giorgio Maggiore, directly across the canal from Piazza San Marco, has a double façade, a dome, and towering bell tower that are reflected in the water, enhancing the drama of the perfectly ordered building.

Thank you, Lord, for the pleasure we receive from
living and working in pleasant structures.

In 1979 Mozart's opera *Don Giovanni* was filmed against three of Palladio's buildings: Villa Rotonda and Teatro Olimpico in Vicenza and Villa La Malcontenta in Mira-Venezia.

Women Artists

*"Who can find a virtuous wife? For her worth is far above rubies ...
[She] willingly works with her hands."*
Proverbs 31:10,13b

Being a wife and mother or a nun were the only career options for women in the 16th century when three extraordinary women suddenly appeared in the art world. Sofonisba Anguissola was the first female Italian painter to be internationally recognized. Born into a noble family of Cremona, she was the eldest of seven children, all involved with the arts. After studying with local artists, she went to Rome where she met Michelangelo. In 1559 she moved to Spain to be court portraitist for King Philip II. Later, living in Genoa with her second husband, the Flemish artist Anthony Van Dyck visited her and drew her picture in his sketchbook with notes of her advice on painting.

Lavinia Fontana was born in Bologna, daughter of successful painter Prospero Fontana. In 1577 she married a wealthy artist, Gian Paolo Zappi, who recognized her enormous talent and was content to paint backgrounds for some of her paintings. She painted portraits, mostly of the aristocracy. Her public commissions included paintings of religious and mythological subjects. She received commissions for large altarpieces for churches in Spain and Italy. Pope Clement VIII invited her to become an official painter to the papal court.

Artemisia Gentileschi, daughter of painter Orazio Gentileschi, was born in Rome in 1593. Early she learned to mix paints, make varnishes, and prepare canvasses for her father. She had almost no life outside her father's studio and was raped by her art tutor when she was a teenager. As the abuse continued, she brought charges against him. Legal records still exist of the long court battle in which her tormentor, Agostino Tassi, was declared guilty of rape, a surprising outcome in that time. He was sentenced to years in prison, but he served very little time, as he was needed to finish some frescoes for a cardinal. Her most famous surviving paintings are *Susannah and the Elders* and several versions of *Judith Beheading Holofernes*.

*Father, thank you for courageous, talented women
who use their talents in positive ways.*

Sofonisba Anguissola lived to be 93 and died in Palermo in 1625.

Caravaggio

"Light is sweet; how pleasant to see a new day dawning."
Ecclesiastes 11:7 (NLT)

Michelangelo Merisi da Caravaggio is known by the name of his home town, Caravaggio, near Milan. A dark-haired man with brown eyes and heavy brows, he sometimes used himself as the model for a beheaded John the Baptist, a popular painting theme. Born in 1573, 10 years after the death of Michelangelo, Caravaggio used peasants and people from the streets as models for his unusual interpretations of biblical stories.

Caravaggio painted religious themes with great realism. He often painted in the dark with only a candle to illuminate the face of the model. With this technique, he produced disturbing results with light and dark. Plotting light sources was important to him. To paint the story of the conversion of St. Paul, he searched Rome for the most beautiful piebald horse he could find. In the painting, Paul lies on the ground, struck blind by the bright light that the viewer perceives as it bounces off the horse's white flanks. When criticized for making the horse more prominent than the saint, Caravaggio explained, "It's the light that is important." He wouldn't have known how else to suggest God's presence without painting bright light.

His strange personality, which seemed to thrive in dark places, made him a recluse. Once when he had avoided people for months, he went to an inn for dinner where he met some young men. Before he realized what was happening, he quarreled, fought, and killed one person. This lethal mistake made him a fugitive for the rest of his life. Pursued by legal forces, Caravaggio traveled toward Rome hoping to receive a papal pardon. He died at the age of 37, an outlaw whose work changed the course of European art.

*Gracious Father, help us to develop and use
the talents you give us. May we live good lives.*

Caravaggio's use of light influenced
Rembrandt, Rubens, and Velasquez.

Bernini, the Sculptor

"Great is the LORD, and greatly to be praised
In the city of our God, In His holy mountain."
Psalm 48:1

One houseguest from California announced her purpose for coming to Rome: "I want to see everything that Bernini sculpted or designed!" so I took her to see the incomparable *Ecstasy of St. Teresa* in the Church of Santa Maria della Vittoria.

Gian Lorenzo Bernini was the son of a Florentine sculptor who worked in the court of the Bourbons in Naples in the last decades of the 16th century. His mother was a Neapolitan. Combined in him were the Tuscan flair for design and the Neapolitan passion for life. As a child, Bernini was considered an artistic prodigy. When he was 8 years old, he sculpted a marble head of a boy that was so well done, people could not believe his genius. Adult sculptors said he knew instinctively what it had taken them decades to learn. For three years Bernini spent each day in the Vatican, sketching ancient marble statues and modern paintings. Years later he told the French Academy in Paris that all French art students should study in Rome so they could draw the ancient statues and thus learn from the best sculptors of the past.

Bernini considered himself a sculptor. He had a freedom in working with stone that allowed him to work without blocking out the marble. Before beginning work, however, he made innumerable drawings or models in clay, and he worked precisely from his exact mental image. Artists said he worked the hard marble as if it were dough and produced statues that seem to have been cast in bronze. Before he was 17, he had commissions from the papal family. During his long life he worked for eight different popes. A very religious man, he went to mass every day and took communion twice a week. He sculpted saints and sinners, Biblical figures and mythological ones.

Father, thank you for the creative spirit of a genius like Bernini,
whose wonderful art has inspired generations.

The statues in the Fountain of the Four Rivers in Rome's Piazza
Navona were designed by Bernini and executed by his pupils.

Bernini, the Architect

"But will God indeed dwell on the earth? Behold, heaven and the heaven of heavens cannot contain You. How much less this temple which I have built!"
I Kings 8:27

Fortunes of a Roman artist of the 16th and 17th centuries depended on that person's relationship with the pope. Pope Urban VIII said Gian Lorenzo Bernini was born, "for the glory of Rome to illuminate the century." They were great friends and often enjoyed chatting over a meal. He urged Bernini to study painting and architecture because he wanted an artist as versatile as Michelangelo had been 100 years before. Bernini enjoyed combining the strength and beauty of architecture, sculpture, and painting, blending them into a harmonious whole.

Bernini had several commissions in St. Peter's Basilica and eventually became responsible for all work in the great cathedral. The greatest work he did was the design of the canopy over the papal altar, above St. Peter's tomb. Gigantic bronze columns and a bronze canopy required tons of metal. The pope ordered bronze to be taken from the Pantheon and other ancient works. The architectural result of the altar is stunning and gives focus under the dome to the dramatic presence of the pope on high holy days. In the apse is St. Peter's Chair, designed by Bernini. He was responsible for planning the four great statues that stand in the four piers that support St. Peter's dome. He designed the papal stairway and decorations on the piers of the main apse of the church. In later years he sculpted several tombs and an equestrian statue of Constantine.

During a short sojourn in Paris to work for King Louis XIV, Bernini made little imprint on the City of Lights, and it made little on him. He thought Paris was ugly and lacked the elegance of Rome where Bernini's masterpieces have embellished and inspired for 400 years.

Father, thank you for artistic inspiration.
Help us to use our creative gifts to honor you and inspire others.

Bernini's tomb is in Rome's Basilica di Santa Maria Maggiore.

English in Italy

"Do not forget to entertain strangers,
for by so doing some have unwittingly entertained angels."
Hebrews 13:2

The English and Italians have long had a mutual fascination with each other. Two thousand years ago, British slaves were sold in Roman markets. Short, swarthy Latins thought tall, blonde Anglos looked like angels. The Caesars and their armies conquered Britain for its tin and copper. Ancient Roman ruins can be studied in Britain in archeological remains of forts, towns, the Roman bath in Bath, and Hadrian's Wall. Through the years Brits have come to Italy for warmer weather, its art, and for the relaxed life they enjoy there. More than half of William Shakespeare's plays are based on Italian stories. Students worldwide still read of the Italian experiences of Lord Byron, Shelley, Keats, Robert and Elizabeth Browning, and many other English travelers who wrote, illustrated, and published their own travel journals and novels inspired by their grand tours. E.M. Forster captured the excitement of the English in Florence with his novel—which was made into a popular movie—*A Room with a View.*

The enthusiasm with which the British enjoy Italy is displayed in the film *Tea with Mussolini* about British expatriates arrested in Italy during World War II. Even in prison, these ladies still demanded the guards bring their tea at 4 p.m. every day, as was their custom.

Mrs. Armstrong, a British pastor's widow, was the quintessential English tourist who came every fall to Italy and lived until spring's warmth reminded her to return to England. She knew Rome better than most Romans. In downtown Rome, All Saints' Anglican Church on Via Babuino, Babington's Tea Room, and Keats-Shelley Museum on Piazza di Spagna are special to the British. Some of Britain's brightest scholars study at the British Academy. *Zuppa inglese*—or English soup—is a pudding doused with excessive brandy. *Il water closet* is a restroom, and *il water* is a toilet. How curious are the cultural exchanges of these very different, amazing peoples!

Lord of all, thank you for varied customs and cultures
that add to life's excitement.

In 2003 a model of London's Globe Theater was built in a park
in Rome for staging Shakespeare's plays.

John Milton

"Beloved, now we are children of God; and it has not yet been revealed what we shall be, but we know that when He is revealed, we shall be like Him, for we shall see Him as He is."
I John 3:2

One afternoon when we were staying at the Vallombrosa Monastery near Florence, we climbed the hills to look at the tall trees and waterfalls. On a promontory we noticed a shrine with a plaque that related a sad story. The place is called *Massa del Diavolo*, or Devil's Rock, where, according to legend, the devil threw a disturbed monk over the precipice to his death.

Behind the monastery, up a hill, and through beautiful woods is a plain two-story house with a fine view of the monastery and peaceful valley. Here English poet John Milton spent time in a retreat. He took a tour of Europe when he was 30 years old. In 15 months of travel and study, he gained information on which he drew for the rest of his life. Milton was a Puritan, a deeply religious person. His writings were laced with Biblical references and strong, positive theology during a time when religious and political struggles divided England among Puritans, the Church of England, and the Crown. His poems and writings pulse with, in his own words to define a good book, "the precious lifeblood of a master spirit."

Milton's unhappy personal life was not reflected in his writings. His first wife left him after two months of marriage. His second wife died after 16 months of marriage. His third marriage lasted 11 years, until his death. Milton's work and constant study strained his weak eyes. By the time he was 44 years old, he was blind. It's thought he dictated his later writings to his daughters. As I stood at Milton's House at Vallombrosa, I thought of his sonnet *On His Blindness*. Unlike the distraught monk of long ago, Milton needed no escape of life's despair. His faith did not diminish during his blind years, but he accepted his physical limitation as a challenge to spiritual growth.

Great Creator, thank you for physical and spiritual vision
to see your wondrous creation and love.

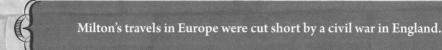

Milton's travels in Europe were cut short by a civil war in England.

John Keats

"Beautiful in elevation, The joy of the whole earth,
Is Mount Zion on the sides of the north, The city of the great King."
Psalm 48:2

Born in London in 1795, John Keats was the son of the manager of a livery stable. His mother was an innkeeper's daughter. Keats studied medicine and passed his examinations, but never practiced medicine because he had decided to be a poet. His first volume, *Poems*, was published in 1817 and dedicated to his friend Leigh Hunt, a poet and newspaper editor of liberal political views. In 1818 Keats published his second volume, *Endymion*, a long mythological story in verse about a beautiful boy in love with the goddess of the moon. It begins with the familiar words: "A thing of beauty is a joy forever." English critics ridiculed Endymion as the work of a lower-class poet, and Keats was sure the scathing criticism had ruined his future as a poet.

After contracting tuberculosis from caring for his brother, this frail young man went to Italy, hoping warmer weather would help him recover from his illness. He lived in a house at 26 Piazza di Spagna, by the Spanish Steps in Rome, and which now houses the Keats-Shelley Museum. The small room in which he died is now lined with copies of his letters and letters of some close friends. On display are several drawings and portraits by his friend, Joseph Severn, who prepared meals for Keats and cared for him until the young poet's death. On the mantle, which was installed when the house was built in 1715, is a copy of Keat's handwritten *Endymion*. The poet Amy Lowell gave the original to Harvard University's library.

Some thought Keats' disappointment at the critical reception of his work weakened his condition, and one friend, the poet Percy Bysshe Shelley, even went so far as to blame his death on negative reviews of *Endymion*.

Loving Father, thank you for beautiful words and thoughts
that lift our souls to you. Help us avoid being too critical of others.

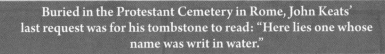

Buried in the Protestant Cemetery in Rome, John Keats'
last request was for his tombstone to read: "Here lies one whose
name was writ in water."

Margaret Fuller

"That which has been is what will be, That which is done is what will be done,
And there is nothing new under the sun."
Ecclesiastes 1:9

"Can you tell me where Piazza Margaret Fuller is?" asked a tourist. I had never heard of Margaret Fuller, though she was famous enough to have a Roman piazza named for her. The tourist launched into a description of the first American woman foreign correspondent.

Interpreting Italy for American readers in the mid-19th century, Margaret Fuller sent reports to the *New York Tribune*. Editor Horace Greeley liked her interpretations and didn't mind printing the work of a woman.

"Who can ever be alone for a moment in Italy? Every stone has a voice, every grain of dust seems instilled with spirit from the past," wrote Fuller. She had great enthusiasm for Rome, which she expressed eloquently.

A clever woman, Fuller used her wits to protect herself in times of danger. While traveling to Rome from Rieti, she entered an area where Garibaldi's troops were known to be. Tales of brutality had gone before them, and people were afraid the accusations were true. At a small inn where she stopped for lunch, some soldiers of Garibaldi approached. The innkeeper was very upset, afraid of the damage they might do. Fuller ordered the innkeeper to feed the men at her expense. Noise and confusion turned to courtly bows. Expecting fear and resentment, Garibaldi's soldiers were met with hospitality and gentility, and they responded with gratitude.

Returning to America after many years in Italy, Fuller traveled with her young son and husband. In sight of the American coast, the ship was pounded by a sudden storm on July 19, 1850. Cargo included 150 tons of Carrara marble, which crashed through the ship, helping to sink it when it hit a reef. Many passengers were drowned in the tragedy, including Fuller and her family.

Father, thank you for courageous people who attempt challenging tasks.

Fuller had long been writing a history of Italy;
the manuscript was lost at sea when she died.

Robert and Elizabeth Barrett Browning

"Love never fails."
I Corinthians 13:8a

Tall, handsome energetic Robert Browning was practical, gregarious, and self-assured. The son of a banker, he received a good education from excellent tutors who taught him Latin, Greek, French, music, and other studies. He was impressed with the works of Keats and Shelley and decided to become a poet. By the age of 20 he published his first poem anonymously. He spent a year in Italy and returned to England. He began correspondence with Elizabeth Barrett, an invalid poet, whose work he admired. Elizabeth's stern father frowned on the poet's interest in his beautiful, intelligent daughter. The couple married without her father's consent and moved to Florence where they lived for 15 happy years. At the age of 43 Elizabeth bore a son. Her health improved dramatically.

The cultural environment of Florence stimulated the two poets. Many of their poems have Italian settings. In Florence the Brownings lived in a villa known as Casa Guidi. They also visited Rome where places related to their Roman sojourn may still be seen. A plaque on a building near the Spanish Steps indicates it was their residence for awhile.

Elizabeth was a feminist and urged rights for women, working children, and Italians who were living under foreign oppression. Robert called his brown-eyed, brunette beauty, "My little Portuguese." Elizabeth's *Sonnets from the Portuguese* are 44 poems about her growing love for her husband. Of her many poetic works, this collection—especially the poem *How Do I Love Thee?*—is most frequently quoted. Elizabeth is buried in the English cemetery in Florence in a white Carrara marble tomb on which are chiseled words from this most-famous sonnet.

On December 12, 1861, 28 years later, Robert died in Venice in the home of their son. His body was taken to London for burial in Westminster Abbey.

Loving God, thank you for loving us and for broadening our lives through loving relationships.

Robert Browning was known to say, "Italy was my university."

Giuseppe Verdi

"Then a herald cried aloud: 'To you it is commanded, O peoples, nations, and languages, that at the time you hear the sound of the horn, flute, harp, lyre, and psaltery, in symphony with all kinds of music, you shall fall down and worship the gold image that King Nebuchadnezzar has set up.'"
Daniel 3:4-5

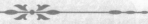

In plays and movies when a happy, enthusiastic family sits at a dinner table and operatic arias soar, we know immediately this is an Italian family. More often than not, the stirring background music is by Giuseppe Verdi, arguably the most recognized Italian composer. Born in Roncole near Parma in 1813, he studied music in the town of Busseto and with Vincenzo Lavigna, a Milanese composer.

His first opera, *Oberto*, was produced in Milan with some success. His next work, a comic opera, was a failure. His wife and two children died, and he decided he would not be able to compose again, but the director of Milan's prestigious opera persuaded him to write the music for *Nabucco*, the story of the Babylonian captivity of the Jews and of their trials under Nebuchadnezzar, *Nabucco* in Italian. When the Italian public heard the words of several choruses, they adopted them as patriotic songs, defying Austrian rule in northern Italy.

Verdi wrote *Rigoletto, Il Trovatore,* and *La Traviata* between 1851 and 1853. These three works brought him international fame and remain the most frequently performed Italian operas. In all, he wrote 25 operas.

As Verdi developed his style, he gave the orchestra greater prominence in his works with strong, recurring musical themes. Perhaps his most popular opera is *Aida*, written in 1871 as Italy was becoming a modern nation. The opera was composed to celebrate the opening of the Suez Canal and was first performed in Cairo. Again, he used patriotic themes and love of country to appeal to the audience. Though he wrote other musical compositions, his forte was grand opera with Italian lyrics. Through his music, he helped shape the Italians' desire for national unity. When Verdi died in Milan on January 27, 1901, the nation mourned his passing.

Maker of sound, thank you for music that lifts our souls and expresses our feelings.

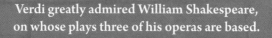

Verdi greatly admired William Shakespeare, on whose plays three of his operas are based.

Pinocchio

*"Do not be wise in your own eyes; Fear the LORD and depart from evil. It will be health to
your flesh, And strength to your bones."*
Proverbs 3:7-8

Everyone enjoys a story about a poor boy who succeeds when the world is against him, but a wooden puppet who despite all odds becomes a real boy? Carlo Lorenzini, a distinguished Italian writer and journalist, fashioned a charming, imaginative tale of how Geppetto, a lonely old man, carved a wooden puppet that learned how to become a real boy. Writing under the pseudonym C. Collodi, the name of his village between Florence and Pisa, Lorenzini's short story was printed in July 1881 in *Il Giornale dei Bambini*, The Newspaper for Children.

The puppet's story, *The Adventures of Pinocchio*, was told in serial segments, and the characters represent good and bad human beings: a fairy, talking animals and birds, bad boys who become donkeys, a talking cricket, a fish one kilometer long, and a puppet who must learn responsibility before he can become a "real boy." The name *Pinocchio* is slang for "pine nut," meaning a rigid person, bound by rules.

One adventure concerns Pinocchio learning the value of money. At the insistence of a fox and a cat, Pinocchio stupidly "plants" four copper coins in a field so they will grow into money trees. Robbed, he learns that money does not grow on trees.

When the puppet lies, his nose grows. When he confesses, his nose shortens. He runs away with truant boys, skips school, and eventually turns into a dancing donkey in a traveling show. The story teaches that to grow into a mature person, a child must go to school; enjoy learning; and be obedient, thoughtful of others, and responsible with money and duties. A good boy honors his family and respects others. Written in elegant Italian, this fanciful story, enjoyed by parents and children, is a masterpiece of Italian literature.

*Thank you, Lord, for parents and teachers who help
children become mature, responsible people.*

The village of Collodi is near Lucca, and visitors—especially those
with children—should stop at *Il Parco di Pinocchio*.

Maria Montessori

"Train up a child in the way he should go, And when he is old he will not depart from it."
Proverbs 22:6

At the Montessori School in Perugia our four-year-old daughter Peggy began to speak Italian. While my husband and I learned verb conjugations, our daughter was playing with Italian children and painlessly absorbing *la bella lingua*. When we moved to Rome the following year, Peggy entered our neighborhood Montessori School. Her teacher had known Maria Montessori, Italy's first female doctor, who channeled medical skills into childhood education.

Montessori was born near Ancona in 1870. Her father wanted her to be a teacher, but she chose to study medicine at the University of Rome. She endured difficult requirements as the only female medical student. Peggy's teacher told me that a small fence was erected around Montessori's desk in a back corner of the room, separating her from males. Because it was not proper to dissect a cadaver in mixed company, she worked in the lab alone at night. Sometime during her studies or early career, she bore a son, Mario Montessori, whom she sent into the country to a wet nurse. Not until her own mother's death did she publicly acknowledge her son, who was 15 at the time. She never revealed the name of the father.

In the early 20th century it was very difficult for a female to practice medicine in Italy. Young Dr. Montessori became involved in the health and education of poor children, many of whom had learning disabilities or handicaps. She set up a school for poor children in Rome's working class neighborhood of San Lorenzo.

After she lectured in the United States, many Montessori schools were established. She represented Italy in an international women's congress in Berlin and charmed everyone with her gracious presence and innovative ideas. She wrote to a friend, "So here I am: famous! It is not very difficult, as you see. I am not famous because of my skill or my intelligence, but for my courage and indifference towards everything."

Father, thank you for good teachers who help shape our lives.

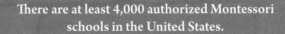

There are at least 4,000 authorized Montessori
schools in the United States.

Celebrities

"He who has the Son has life; he who does not have the Son of God does not have life."
I John 5:12

Blockbuster films were being made in Rome, the European film capital during the 1960s. Rome's English-language newspaper and Italian papers printed reports and photographs of celebrities in fashionable restaurants and lounges of the city.

The rich and famous are seen often in Rome. One rainy day on Via Condotti, I exchanged smiles and nods with actress Janet Leigh. While paying Peggy's tuition at American Overseas School of Rome, Dub stood in line and chatted with parent Jack Palance. Several times at an American Women's Association luncheon I ate at a table with Burt Lancaster's wife. Also at those luncheons I met Claire Boothe Luce, American ambassador to Italy after World War II; advice columnist Abigail Van Buren; writer Luigi Barzini; and actress Gina Lollabrigida. At a restaurant in Piazza Navona, we spoke to Norman Rockwell and his wife who were at the next table. At an American Men's Club luncheon, Dub chatted a moment with Lyndon Johnson, both native Texans. When Jimmy and Rosalind Carter came to Rome, we were asked by the Embassy to invite at least 100 guests to a reception in the gardens of the American Consulate. We stood close enough for Dub to tell the Carters that their Atlanta pastor was a friend of ours. We have some wonderful pictures of Queen Elizabeth II, dressed in yellow, getting out of her limousine and walking up the steps of the Victor Emmanuel Monument.

Once I said to an Italian who was drinking an espresso next to me in a coffee bar, "The king of Denmark is in town today. I hope I see him." Accustomed to famous faces, this jaded Roman said, "I wouldn't walk across the street to see a prince or king or anybody."

Thank you, Father, for interesting people who enhance life for us all.

Federico Fellini coined the term *paparazzi* in his 1960 film *La Dolce Vita*. It's from an Italian slang word for a noisy, buzzing mosquito.

Section IV
Faithful Italy

The Cross

"But God forbid that I should boast except in the cross of our Lord Jesus Christ,
by whom the world has been crucified to me, and I to the world."
Galatians 6:14

A cross is the most recognized symbol of the Christian faith, and they are everywhere in Italy: on the roofs and domes of churches, carved into doors, designed into pulpits, and always on the altar. Many Italians wear a cross or a crucifix around their necks. The crucifix immediately identifies the person as a baptized believer.

From a tool of torture and death, the cross has become a symbol of the Passion. Crucifixion was a form of cruel punishment perfected by the Persians, adapted by the Carthaginians, and adopted by the Romans when they conquered the territories of Alexander the Great. Before a criminal was crucified, he was usually flogged with whip until his body was lacerated. The face was not spared. Sometimes a victim lost an eye or ear. Always he lost much blood. Sometimes the accused carried the crossbeam to the place of crucifixion. The hands and feet were either bound to the cross with ropes or the limbs were nailed on. Often nails were put through the wrist, as there was more flesh to hold the body's weight through the wrists than through the hands. Death by crucifixion was agonizing, often taking days.

The sign of the cross indicates the devout person is praying and honoring the crucified Christ. It is made by the right hand, with fingers cupped. A Catholic quickly touches the forehead, moves to mid-chest, touches the left shoulder, then the right shoulder. A Catholic makes the sign of the cross when a funeral procession passes by, when he hears tragic news of dear friends or relatives, when entering the church, when seeing the pope, when concluding a prayer or beginning a meal, and when warding off evil. With upraised hand, a priest makes the sign of the cross as he blesses his parishioners. Italian Catholics use it naturally to express their faith.

Father, thank you for your sinless Son
who died for our sins on a shameful cross.

A crucifix is a cross with a representation of Jesus' crucified body.

St. Mary

*"The virgin's name was Mary. And having come in, the angel said to her, 'Rejoice, highly
favored one, the Lord is with you; blessed are you among women!'"*
Luke 1:27b-28

Italians honor the Virgin Mary, mother of Jesus Christ. Her name is uttered in several forms in prayer or as an expression of great emotion: *Madonna! Santa Virgine! Santa Madre di Dio!* Shrines to Mary are on the corners of buildings at street intersections, and hundreds of churches and places are named for her.

Mary is honored for her purity, her compassion, and her access to her Son. Roman Catholics feel comfortable praying to a loving mother who understands their weaknesses and dreams. They believe this special woman is in heaven, interceding for all believers. In every Catholic church, the faithful adore her images as they look to her for protection. Renaissance artists depicted her as the Queen of Heaven, enthroned by Christ's side, crowned as co-regent with the Son of God. Catholics honor Mary by saying the rosary, a designation for both this devotional prayer and the beads themselves.

Biblical references to Mary are few in comparison to the authority she has been awarded in Roman Catholic theology. Luke tells of Gabriel's annunciation to Mary that she would bear a son and call his name Jesus and of Mary's visit with Elizabeth, the birth in Bethlehem, the adoration of the shepherds, the presentation of the holy family in the temple, and the family's journey to Jerusalem for the Feast of the Passover when Jesus was 12. Matthew recounts the visit of the Wise Men; the killing of the innocents by Herod; and the flight of Mary, Joseph, and the baby to Egypt. John remembers when Jesus spoke to Mary from the Cross. All these stories are depicted in the great art of Italy's churches and museums.

Mary is honored throughout the year in several holidays. Both secular and religious Italians set aside August 15, The Assumption of Mary or *Ferragosto*, as the last summer opportunity for a day in the sun.

*Dear Lord, thank you for the willingness of Mary to bear
and mother the Son of God.*

Some of Europe's great churches are named for Mary. Notre Dame in Paris,
Santa Maria Maggiore in Rome, and Santa Maria degli Angel below
Assisi are only a few.

St. Joseph

"And you, fathers, do not provoke your children to wrath,
but bring them up in the training and admonition of the Lord."
Ephesians 6:4

Italian Father's Day is March 19, St. Joseph's Day. Joseph of Nazareth—the husband of Mary—loved and taught the young Jesus. He is honored as a godly parent. Churches named for Joseph have special celebrations to remember his saint's day. Fried pastries called *bignè di San Giuseppe* are similar to doughnut balls, sprinkled with sugar. Sometimes a parade with his statue is part of the celebration.

Italian fathers have a certain role to maintain. They seem to take seriously the education of their children. More and more, as incomes rise, fathers are taking their children on vacations that they consider educational. One of our Italian neighbors bought a camping trailer and worked out a plan where family vacations would combine experiences in Europe as well as relaxation at popular Italian beaches. *Papà* often leaves the religious instruction to *mamma*, but when special functions—such as baptisms, first communions, marriages, and funerals—are on the agenda, he can be the stalwart head of the family, approving proper procedures and paying the bills for the family celebrations that those functions include. On Sundays and holidays many parents and children enjoy an outing together. Often, especially in small towns, mothers walk in a park with the small children while fathers talk with friends in the piazza, play a game of bocci under the trees, or sit in front of the bar and have a drink.

Papà—said with an accent on the last syllable—is a familiar version of the more formal *padre*. When talking about their father to others, many people use *padre*. Italian children call their father *babbo*, similar to "daddy." *Papa*—spoken with equal emphasis on both syllables—is the word for "pope," the Holy Father.

Lord, thank you for the example of Joseph
and for godly fathers who love and protect their children.

**Burying a small statue of St. Joseph is said to enlist
the saint's help in selling a property.**

St. John the Baptist

"So he sent and had John beheaded in prison. And his head was brought on a platter and given to the girl, and she brought it to her mother."
Matthew 14:10-11

John the Baptist's birth is celebrated in Italy on June 24, one of two feast days for the saint. Paintings in many churches and museums depict the visit of Mary of Nazareth with her cousin Elisabeth. On that occasion, the unborn John leapt in his mother Elisabeth's womb when Mary, carrying the Messiah, arrived for a visit. Both women were experiencing miraculous pregnancies. Elisabeth was an old woman and Mary was a virgin. Elisabeth and Zechariah, the aged parents of the miracle child, named him John, as an angel had directed them to do. The two mothers and the young cousins, John and Jesus, are depicted in many works of art.

The gospel of Mark begins with the preaching of John the Baptist: "Repent, and follow the gospel" (1:15). Crowds of people walked from cities and towns in Judea to be baptized by John in the Jordan River. When Jesus asked John to baptize him, John said he was not worthy. Behind the baptismal font in St. Peter's Basilica is a mosaic of John baptizing Jesus by pouring water on his head. In artistic presentations, John is always wearing a camel-hair skin. Sometimes he holds a staff and scroll with the words *Ecce Agnus Dei*, which means "Behold the Lamb of God."

Because John denounced Herod Antipas for marrying Herodias, his brother's wife, Herodias was determined to have John killed. The prophet was put in prison and remained there until beautiful, sensuous Salome, daughter of Herodias, danced for Herod. In a weak moment, Herod vowed to give her whatever she asked. Instructed by her mother, Salome asked for the head of John the Baptist. Gruesome paintings of the head of the silenced prophet are in every major art gallery in Italy.

Lord, help us to be ever faithful to you.
We know you are with us in all of life's tragedies and joys.

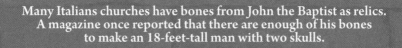

Many Italians churches have bones from John the Baptist as relics.
A magazine once reported that there are enough of his bones
to make an 18-feet-tall man with two skulls.

Simon Peter

"And Jesus, walking by the Sea of Galilee, saw two brothers, Simon called Peter, and Andrew his brother, casting a net into the sea; for they were fishermen. Then He said to them, 'Follow Me, and I will make you fishers of men.' They immediately left their nets and followed Him."

Matthew 4:18-20

Simon was a simple, hard-working fisherman. Jesus gave Simon the name "Peter" when Jesus asked the disciples who they thought he was. Always quick to respond, Simon declared, "'You are the Christ, the Son of the living God.' Jesus answered and said to him, 'Blessed are you, Simon Bar-Jonah, for flesh and blood has not revealed this to you, but My Father who is in heaven. And I also say to you that you are Peter, and on this rock I will build My church, and the gates of Hades shall not prevail against it.'" (Matthew 16:16-18.)

This important verse is inscribed in the Basilica of St. Peter, around the base of the dome over the high altar, high above the tomb of Simon Peter. Literal interpretation gives scriptural authority to the Roman Church for their claim that Peter was the first bishop, or pope, of Rome, a position tradition says he held for 25 years.

Peter, his brother Andrew, James, and John—all fishermen—were the first disciples of Jesus. Once when Jesus walked on the surface of a lake, Peter stepped out of the boat and walked toward the Master, then suddenly began to doubt. Filled with fear, he began to sink. This story of faith is depicted in an ancient Giotto mosaic on the porch of St. Peter's Basilica.

During the Passover supper, Jesus told Peter that he would deny him three times, but Peter was incredulous. Jesus chose Peter, James, and John to pray with him in the Garden of Gethsemane before his crucifixion. During Christ's trial at the palace of the high priest, Peter denied Christ to three different people. In the Vatican Museum is Caravaggio's remarkable painting of Peter denying Christ to a serving girl. For the remainder of his life, the fisherman would regret his cowardly denial of Jesus.

***Forgiving Father, help us to be strong
in our profession of faith in Jesus Christ, our savior.***

Three churches in Rome are named for Peter: San Pietro in Montorio on the Janiculum Hill, San Pietro in Carcere, in the Mamertine Prison near the Forum, and San Pietro in Vaticano , where—according to tradition—he was buried.

Peter the Apostle

"Then Peter said to them, 'Repent, and let every one of you be baptized in the name of Jesus Christ for the remission of sins; and you shall receive the gift of the Holy Spirit.'"

Acts 2:38

On June 29, Feast Day for Saints Peter and Paul, the statue of St. Peter in the Basilica of St. Peter is embellished with jewels and dressed in an elaborate robe. Under the high altar of the basilica, two levels below ground, is the tomb of St. Peter. Excavations after World War II determined the place was definitely the burial place of an important person. Twelve people were entombed around Peter's casket, placed like petals around the center of a daisy.

From gospel accounts, we know that Peter was not present at the crucifixion. He was the first to see the risen Christ after Mary Magdalene told the disciples she had seen Him. Peter was in the upper room when Christ appeared to the disciples. On other occasions Peter saw the risen Christ and witnessed Christ's ascension into heaven. On the Feast of Pentecost, Peter and the others received the Holy Spirit, and they spoke in other languages to the pilgrim crowds. Peter preached, and 3,000 people were saved. The volatile fisherman had become an eloquent preacher and leader. He worked miracles.

From Acts, we know King Herod Agrippa I had Peter imprisoned about A.D. 42, but a miraculous escape—attributed to the help of an angel—set Peter free. Some scholars think he went into areas that are in the modern country of Turkey. Because of archeological evidence, as well as writings of the early church, Roman Catholics are positive that Peter went to Rome. Roman tradition says that Peter and Paul were imprisoned in the Mamertine Prison during persecutions under Emperor Nero. Tradition says the apostles were executed between A.D. 64 and 68. Every year hundreds of thousands of faithful Roman Catholics pray in the elaborate St. Peter's Basilica before the tomb of the simple fisherman from Galilee.

Gracious God, we thank you that Christian faith becomes stronger with life's testing.

In art, St. Peter is often depicted holding the keys to heaven.

St. Longinus

"Then the soldiers came and broke the legs of the first and of the other who was crucified with Him. But when they came to Jesus and saw that He was already dead, they did not break His legs. But one of the soldiers pierced His side with a spear, and immediately blood and water came out."

John 19:32-34

In the four supporting columns in St. Peter's Basilica are statues of the people involved in the crucifixion of Christ: Veronica and the legendary veil with the likeness of Christ, Helen—the mother of Constantine—and parts of the true cross, the Apostle Andrew and his skull, and Longinus and the spear with which he pierced Christ's side. All four gospels mention the soldiers who crucified Christ, who divided his garments among themselves, and made remarks about him. After the darkness preceding his death and the earthquake, the centurion is reported to have said, "Truly this Man was the Son of God!" (Mark 15:39).

In the apocryphal Acts of Pilate, the centurion who pierced the side of Christ was named Longinus. Another apocryphal version gives the name Longinus to the centurion who realized that Jesus was the Son of God. Some scholars think there were two soldiers, but some believe only one soldier was responsible for both the piercing of the side of Christ and the declaration of His divinity. The Venerable Bede wrote that Longinus was martyred for his faith at Caesarea in Cappadocia in A.D. 58.

The drama of the crucifixion has caused many novelists to construct stories about the Lord's robe, for which the soldiers gambled, and for the centurion's lance that pierced his side. In the film version of Lloyd Douglas' novel *The Robe*, Richard Burton played the part of the centurion in charge of the execution. In these stories the life of the centurion was changed when he realized that truly Jesus was the Son of God.

During New Testament times, crucifixion was reserved for non-Romans. Beheading—swifter, more humane—was for Roman citizens. Thus Christ and later Peter, Andrew, and countless other believers were crucified.

Lord, people come to faith in you in different ways. Help us to see your glory.

Longinus derives from the Greek word for "lance."

Easter

"Pilate answered and said to them again, 'What then do you want me to do with Him whom you call the King of the Jews?' So they cried out again, 'Crucify Him!'"
Mark 15:12-13

Christians throughout the world observe Holy Week with throngs of tourists visiting Italy to commemorate Christ's death and resurrection. In Rome, during the Thursday evening service in the Basilica of St. John in Lateran, the pope washes the feet of 12 men and serves communion. The Last Supper and agony in the garden are commemorated.

Good Friday, the Friday before Easter, is the day on which the crucifixion of Jesus is remembered. From the 16th century until 1955, Rome's Good Friday services took place in the morning. In 1955 Pope Pius XII decreed that the service be held in the afternoon or evening. The Stations of the Cross are remembered in the Colosseum, where large crowds gather and priests from many nations read scriptures. When he is physically able to do so, the pope carries a cross in this dramatic service.

One year my husband and I attended the Good Friday mass in St. Peter's, surrounded by 10,000 people from all over the world. International clergy prayed and read Bible passages in Italian and in 18 other languages. Pope Paul VI gave a homily on the Passion of the Christ. When it was time for the communion, dozens of priests walked down the aisles with baskets of communion wafers. People began to push others aside and to crawl over chairs to get to the priests, impatient to leave after a very long service.

On Holy Saturday, pilgrims and tourists see as many sights as they can. In churches, the liturgical color of the day is black. No bells are rung. The organ is silent. After the evening service, the altar is left bare, and the empty Tabernacle is left open.

Easter Sunday the pope says mass for the crowds of people and delivers a televised message, *Urbi et Orbi*, which means "from the city to the world." Numerous doves are released and fly around the square as the faithful look heavenward. It is a thrilling moment.

We are grateful, loving Lord, for the sacrificial gift of Christ's life for us and for His example of how to live and how to die.

Good Friday has been celebrated at least since the fourth century when Emperor Constantine ruled.

Saul of Tarsus

"As he journeyed he came near Damascus, and suddenly a light shone around him from heaven. Then he fell to the ground, and heard a voice saying to him, 'Saul, Saul, why are you persecuting Me?'"
Acts 9:3-4

One of the most influential men who ever lived, Saul—who became the apostle Paul—was the son of Jewish parents and a Roman citizen, born in the free city of Tarsus, in what is now southern Turkey. The bright young Jew went to Jerusalem to study with Gamaliel, the most noted rabbi of his day. Because every Hebrew male learned a trade, Saul worked as a tentmaker, making sails, tents, and working with leather. Throughout his life, tent-making was his source of income and the means by which he met people and made friends.

Saul grew into a rigid Pharisee, legalistic and forceful in his interpretation of the Mosaic Law. During the stoning of Stephen, he stood by, holding the cloaks of those who cast the stones. On his way to Damascus to arrest Christians who had fled there, Saul had a vision in which a bright light blinded him and he heard the voice of Christ. Saul continued the journey to Damascus where Ananias told him the Lord had revealed that Saul would preach the gospel to the Gentiles. Saul believed in Jesus and immediately received his sight.

No person in the empire was better equipped to evangelize the Greeks and Romans. Saul—who now was called Paul—preached and established many churches on three missionary journeys through the eastern end of the Mediterranean. To churches and individuals he wrote many letters, which comprise a large portion of the New Testament. Of his experiences Paul reported to the church in Corinth that he had been beaten with rods three times; stoned once; suffered shipwreck three times; spent a night floating in the open sea; suffered from hunger, thirst, cold, and nakedness; and had been in great peril on many occasions. Paul's optimistic, Christian faith enabled him to interpret all of his experiences in positive ways. Daily he experienced God's love and grace.

Father, thank you for Paul,
for his ministry, and for his writings that instruct us in faith.

The name *Paul* is the Gentile equivalent of the Jewish "Saul."

Paul the Apostle

*"For I long to see you, that I may impart to you some spiritual gift,
so that you may be established."*
Romans 1:11

Paul had long wanted to go to Rome. Because of his mission to the Gentiles, Paul was attacked by a mob in Jerusalem around A.D. 58. He was put under the protective custody of Roman soldiers and sent to Governor Felix at Caesarea, where his trial was delayed two years until Festus succeeded Felix. As a Roman citizen Paul demanded, and was granted, a trial in Rome. En route to Rome, he was shipwrecked off the coast of Malta. Another ship picked up the survivors, and once in Rome Paul was allowed to live in his own rented house until his trial before Caesar Nero. Many legends abound concerning the last years of his life.

According to Clement of Rome, who wrote 30 years after Paul's death, Paul was acquitted by the emperor and traveled to Spain to preach. If Clement was correct, Paul possibly revisited Ephesus, Macedonia, and other parts of Greece between A.D. 63 and 67. In this tradition, he was arrested again at Troas and returned to Rome where he was imprisoned in the Mamertine Prison.

Roman traditions say Paul and Peter were executed on the same day, June 29—their saint day—but some historians dispute this. According to tradition, Peter was crucified upside down, a request he made so as not to be crucified in the same position as his Lord. Paul, being a Roman citizen, was given the more merciful death by decapitation. Christian women of the Lucina family came for his body and buried it in their family cemetery on Via Ostiense. Shortly afterward, a small shelter was erected over the grave. During the reign of Emperor Constantine, the Basilica of St. Paul was built. In the Abbey of the Three Fountains, where Paul was executed, and in the Basilica of St. Paul Outside the Walls, where he was buried, there is always a sense of profound peace.

Father, help us to be strong in our faith and witness like Paul.

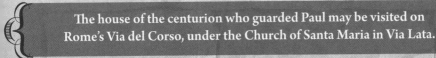

**The house of the centurion who guarded Paul may be visited on
Rome's Via del Corso, under the Church of Santa Maria in Via Lata.**

The Passion

"So Pilate, wanting to gratify the crowd, released Barabbas to them; and he delivered Jesus, after he had scourged Him, to be crucified."
Mark 15:15

The Passion of Christ—Mel Gibson's religious blockbuster—was filmed in Matera, a small hilltop town in Basilicata in the instep of the Italian boot. For 2,000 years the Materese lived in cave dwellings, scooped out of the hillsides. In the back of most of the caves the peasant dug out a shelf, a manger, to hold hay for the animals that lived in the same cave. The hill town makes for a dramatic setting with its cave homes, hills, and rocky cliffs and resembles what Jerusalem might have looked like during the time of Christ. In November 2002, when the film crew arrived, 20,000 locals auditioned to be extras. Six hundred swarthy Mediterranean-looking people were chosen.

Locals talk about the special effects and filming of the scourging. A government official who portrayed a disciple said there were 20 barrels of "blood" kept on hand in a cave. Between each shooting, make-up artists rearranged the hair of the Christ and applied "blood" from a squeeze bottle. One actor said he had to wash his hair 20 times with dish detergent to clean it from the shoe polish and mud that was matted into his hair for a messy scene.

After viewing the film, the pope said he approved. The mayor and community leaders have been quoted as saying they had no idea the film would be such a commercial success. Seizing on the financial possibilities, the Matera Tourist Office began taking bookings for tours of film locations for the Last Supper and the crucifixion. The town's best hotel, Albergo Italia, began booking the room where Gibson stayed. Restaurants and bed and breakfasts were opened in the former cave homes. Near the ravine, a desolate spot where the crucifixion was staged, two local men carve paperweights and crucifixes for souvenirs.

Father, we know that the suffering of the Christ was unimaginably cruel. We are grateful for His sacrifice

Film extras were paid 60 to 90 euros a day.

St. Praxedes

"To all who are in Rome, beloved of God, called to be saints: Grace to you and peace from God our Father and the Lord Jesus Christ."
Romans 1:7

Stepping into the Church of St. Praxedes is like stepping back 500 years. This well-loved parish church has been used continuously since it was built by Pope Paschal I in the early ninth century. Located one short block from the busy Via Merulana, on a side street near the Basilica of Santa Maria Maggiore, this small, historic church is one of the loveliest in Rome. *Santa Prassede,* as it is known locally, is the stational church for a special vesper service the day after Palm Sunday.

According to legend, the original church on the site, which still stood in 499, was built over the house where Praxedes lived and sheltered persecuted Christians. Soldiers discovered 23 Christians in her home and killed them before her eyes. She collected their blood with a sponge and placed it in a well that later became her own tomb. In the center of the nave, a circular porphyry slab marks the tomb. Like many of Italy's old churches, St. Praxedes has beautiful, elevated frescoes that are in need of restoration. But its Chapel of St. Zeno—decorated with brightly colored mosaic stones—is as colorful as the day it was finished. Romans call the chapel "the garden of paradise." Beautiful mosaics, whose designs recount church history, can be best seen with a spotlight, for which there is a small fee.

On the church's walls, many saints and saintly people are pictured. Two figures wear a square halo, symbol of a living, holy person. In the chapel of St. Zeno, the mother of Pope Paschal is depicted with a square halo. The saintly woman was probably still living when the chapel was decorated. In the apse of the church, Pope Paschal, shown with a group of saints, holds the model of his church.

Immortal, invisible, all-loving God,
we honor you when we share the wonder of your love.

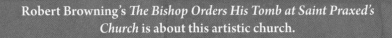

Robert Browning's *The Bishop Orders His Tomb at Saint Praxed's Church* is about this artistic church.

Ancient Churches

The first Christians met in homes, but as the Christian population grew, larger meeting places were required. Sometimes the Christian community was given a defunct pagan sanctuary. A newer, larger building over the original pagan site might conserve the original name. One of the first ancient churches in Rome was Santa Prisca, a house church founded by *Prisca*—or Priscilla as we know her in English—and Aquila, mentioned five times in the New Testament book of Acts and in the epistles of St. Paul.

St. Mary above Minerva used precious marble from the ancient temple of the goddess of wisdom and signified in the name of the church that Mary, mother of Jesus, had triumphed over Minerva. On the Capitoline Hill, the grand temple of Jupiter provided the foundation of another church dedicated to Mary. The Church of St. Mary of the Altar of Heaven commemorates a legend concerning Emperor Augustus Caesar. In a vision he saw above the altar of Jupiter a young woman holding her baby who would rule the world.

Several early churches were named to indicate they were built over the house of a prominent family who willed their property to the congregation that met there. St. Lawrence in Lucina, St. Mary in Cosmedin, and St. Mary in Dominica are such churches. The imperial city's cemeteries, tombs, and catacombs were located "outside the walls," and several of the oldest churches of the city were built over the tombs of martyrs buried in these. St. Paul's Outside the Walls is an example.

When the Apostle Paul referred to a church, he meant the congregation, not the building. The modern definition of a building as a "church" was unknown to early Christians, who met wherever they could.

Thank you for faithful Christians who maintain
cherished places of worship as part of their Christian stewardship.

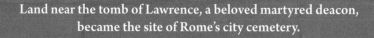

Land near the tomb of Lawrence, a beloved martyred deacon,
became the site of Rome's city cemetery.

St. Perpetua and St. Felicitas

"Yet if anyone suffers as a Christian, let him not be ashamed, but let him glorify God in this matter."
I Peter 4:16

An army officer from the North African city of Carthage, Septimius Severus bought the position of Emperor from the Praetorian Guard in 193. He issued an edict prohibiting Christians from teaching or making converts, hoping to crush the influence of the followers of Christ.

Five Christians in Carthage, including Vibia Perpetua, were condemned to death in the arena because of their faith. She said, "The Holy Spirit has inspired me to pray for nothing but patience under bodily pains." Felicitas, maid-servant of the noble Perpetua and also imprisoned, was eight-months pregnant. Awaiting their execution, the small Christian group prayed, and Felicitas delivered a month early. If the child had not been born, the pregnant woman would have remained in prison and suffered her fate with unknown prisoners. (Perpetua's sister brought up the daughter of Felicitas.)

For the last meal the prisoners celebrated an *agape*, a fellowship meal eaten in remembrance of Jesus. On the day of their execution, the condemned Christians walked to the arena, praying they would be worthy and fearless in their public declaration that Christ is Lord. They sang hymns and encouraged each other. The three men faced the beasts first. A leopard, a bear, and a wild boar attacked them. Perpetua and Felicitas were thrown into the arena and a savage steer badly wounded them. Perpetua walked valiantly back into the arena to be beheaded. She even helped the unskilled gladiator direct the blade to her throat.

On a March day in 203, Perpetua and her companions were slaughtered in the arena in Carthage. Her diary was preserved and represents the triumphant spirit and overcoming faith of early Christians. Tertullian, early church historian, wrote, "O most brave and blessed martyrs, you have gone out of prison rather than into one."

Eternal Father, thank you for true and brave Christians who through the centuries have been courageous witnesses in times of persecution.

St. Perpetua's diary is thought to be the earliest surviving text of a Christian woman.

St. Calixtus

"When Joseph had taken the body, he wrapped it in a clean linen cloth, and laid it in his new tomb which he had hewn out of the rock; and he rolled a large stone against the door of the tomb, and departed."

Matthew 27:59-60

Early Christians wanted to be buried because they anticipated a bodily resurrection while pagan Romans burned their dead. Roman law prohibited burial within the city walls, so burial places were within one to three miles of the city. Wealthy Christians allowed poor Christians to bury their dead in their family plots. A long hall was dug in the ground. The corridor was high enough to bury three or four bodies, one above another in shelves scooped out of the wall. Sometimes another hallway or a stairway was dug so more tombs could be added. Miles of underground burial hallways, several floors underground, created an unseen maze in the campagna, the countryside around the Appian Way. The largest of these is the Catacombs of St. Calixtus.

Calixtus was a Christian slave in Rome in the second century. Entrusted with business dealings, he was accused falsely of fraudulent banking and sent to the mines. The mistress of Emperor Commodus secured his release, and Calixtus returned to Rome. As assistant to Pope Zephyrinus, he was in charge of the catacombs on the Appian Way. Burials were a big responsibility for the rapidly growing Christian community, and the need for tombs was great.

For centuries only the Catacombs of St. Sebastian were known to the public. From ancient writings, scholars knew that other catacombs existed but did not know their locations. Italian archeologist Giovanni Battista De Rossi had studied about many saints who were buried in those lost catacombs. One day in 1854, De Rossi was eating in a restaurant on the Appian Way when he saw an old piece of marble being used as a shelf. On the marble was the inscription *NELIUS Martyr*. He knew immediately it was from the tomb of St. Cornelius, a pope who died in 253 and who was buried in the Catacombs of St. Calixtus. The pope permitted De Rossi to investigate. Since then many catacombs have been discovered.

Lord, thank you for the hope of eternal life in you.

Calixtus succeeded Zephyrinus as pope. He is credited with founding the Church of Santa Maria in Trastevere, the first church building in Rome.

All Saints' Day

"Now when He had taken the scroll, the four living creatures and the twenty-four elders fell down before the Lamb, each having a harp, and golden bowls full of incense, which are the prayers of the saints."

Revelation 5:8

As newcomers to Italy, one of the first phrases we learned was *Domani è festa* or "Tomorrow is a holiday." On All Saints' Day—November 1—schools, banks, offices, and stores close for this national holiday. Churches have special services. Priests honor saints by reading their names and praying. Italians return to their home villages to attend the graves of ancestors and family members.

In the New Testament Paul addressed fellow Christians as "saints." Over the centuries the Roman Catholic Church used the term "saint" to refer to deceased Christians who had been virtuous to a heroic degree. During the Reformation, most Protestants rejected the veneration of saints as not being supported by Scripture. The Roman Catholic Council of Trent in the mid-1500s affirmed the practice of honoring saints and praying to them to ask God for help. The Orthodox Church has similar teachings about saints, though their list of saints is different. Saints are thought to be specialists in certain needs such as St. Christopher for travelers and St. Anthony for children.

The fullest list of saints contains more than 20,000 names. Pope John Paul II canonized hundreds of saints from all over the world. Canonization is the process by which the pope proclaims the sanctity of a deceased person. Usually the process begins 50 years after the person's death. There must be proof of some miracles performed through prayers to the deceased. After a long process of study and testing of evidence, the person is beatified. The decree of beatification is an official declaration that a person lived a holy life and can be considered as a future saint. When the blessed is declared a saint, a ceremony of canonization is held in St. Peter's Basilica. Relatives, acquaintances, and those who have experienced miracles are usually in attendance.

Help us, our Father, to live lives that bless others.

A commemoration of "All Martyrs" began to be celebrated as early as 270.

St. Onofrio

"Blessed are the pure in heart, For they shall see God."
Matthew 5:8

Unexpectedly one day, an invitation arrived for my husband and me to dine with the Prince and Princess Doria at the Doria Palace with other guests. The day of the dinner, it was moved to the Monastery of Sant'Onofrio at the foot of the Janiculum Hill. Founded in 1419 by the Blessed Nicola da Forca Palena as a hermitage for monks of the Hieronymite Order, it was named for St. Onofrio, an Egyptian hermit. For almost 600 years people have enjoyed the monastery's peace and its stunning view of the city.

On a terrace in front of the church are a fountain, ilex trees, and stone benches. A Renaissance portico connects the church and monastery, which preserves the remains of St. Onofrio. Wanting to focus his life on God, the monk lived in a cave in the desert for 60 years. It is said that during that time he never saw nor talked with one human being. He spoke only when he prayed.

In the convent are frescoes of the saint. There are also frescoes of the life of St. Jerome, another member of the Hieronymite Order. One of the scenes is based on a letter to Eustochius, in which Jerome says, "O how often when alone in the desert with the wild beasts and scorpions, half dead with fasting and penance, have I fancied myself a spectator of the sins of Rome, and of the dances of its young women!"

There were no dancing women at the monastery that night, but there were guests who enjoyed the view of Rome in the fading light of day. I sat near the prince, who remarked, "So you are a minister's wife! You don't look like one." Remembering some of the pasty characters in popular novels, I replied, "And what does a minister's wife look like?" He threw up his hands and said, "I don't know. I've never seen one!"

We are glad, our Father, for the many ways people serve you.

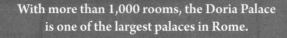

**With more than 1,000 rooms, the Doria Palace
is one of the largest palaces in Rome.**

St. Helen

"And He, bearing His cross, went out to a place called the Place of a Skull,
which is called in Hebrew, Golgotha."
John 19:17

When Constantine became emperor in 306, his mother, Helen—an unusually beautiful and intelligent woman—was immediately raised to a position of great honor. A Christian, she was eager to use her new position to promote the faith. She determined to find the holy places in Palestine where Christ lived and taught. In 326 she went to the Holy Land and founded a basilica on the Mount of Olives.

After Titus destroyed Jerusalem, many people were killed or scattered all over the Mediterranean world. But with the Palestinian culture steeped in oral tradition, the events and places of the ministry of Jesus were remembered by people who remained in the land. Many holy places were marked to secure the public's memory of the places. Undaunted by the difficulties of locating, claiming, and building, Empress Helen—then in her 70s—succeeded in having churches built over Golgotha, the place of the crucifixion, and where Jesus was buried in a tomb of Joseph of Arimathea. In Bethlehem, the cave where Jesus was born and placed in a manger became the site of the impressive Church of the Nativity.

The holy relic that Helen wished to find was the true cross of Christ. Near the site of the crucifixion, remains of an old Roman cross were found. She and others were convinced it was the cross on which Jesus had been crucified. Since then, fragments of this cross have been kept in Rome's Church of the Holy Cross in Jerusalem. Inside the loggia of St. Peter's Basilica is a reliquary, shown on holy days, which is said also to contain fragments of the true cross. In one of the four great pilasters that hold up the dome there is a statue of St. Helen holding the cross.

Lord, thank you for hard challenges,
for demanding work, and for positive results.

To honor his mother Constantine changed
the name of her birthplace to Helenopolis.

Martyrs

"When He opened the fifth seal, I saw under the altar the souls of those who had been slain for the word of God and for the testimony which they held."
Revelation 6:9

Rome's churches preserve the remains of many martyrs. Under every altar are relics of the saints—bones, hair, a skull, an entire body. "Martyr" means "witness," a person who is killed because of his or her beliefs. The first Christian martyr was Stephen, a deacon in the Jerusalem church. His death is described in the book of Acts. James, the brother of John, was beheaded on the orders of King Herod. Another Christian, Antipas, was martyred in Pergamos. He was called "faithful martyr" (Revelation 2:13). The heroic testimonies of martyrs in the church's early centuries were an encouragement to Christians to remain faithful. Before the execution of condemned Christians, people would go to them with special prayer requests, as they knew these wonderful people would soon be in the Lord's presence.

The death of Polycarp, the elderly bishop of Smyrna, was a powerful witness of faith. Eusebius wrote of his burning at the stake: "When the pyre was ready … Polycarp prayed: 'O Father … I bless thee for counting me worthy of this day and hour, that in the number of the martyrs I may partake of Christ's cup, to the resurrection of eternal life of both soul and body in the imperishability that is the gift of the Holy Spirit.'"

The practice of building a chapel or church building over the grave of a martyr became a common practice after Constantine. Having authentic corpses was necessary. This custom of the early Christian church is reflected in the vision recorded in Revelation 6:9, where martyred souls were under the altar. During the Middle Ages, the body of St. Mark was brought to Venice, St. Nicholas to Bari, St. Andrew to Amalfi, St. Stephen to Rome. Pilgrims still make long journeys to pray before the tombs of the saints and martyrs.

Savior and Lord, help us to witness to others of your grace and love.

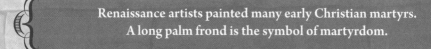

**Renaissance artists painted many early Christian martyrs.
A long palm frond is the symbol of martyrdom.**

St. Valentine

"Love never fails."
I Corinthians 13:8a

St. Valentine's Day honors a priest who lived 18 centuries ago. Legend says Valentine wrote encouraging notes to his parishioners. During a time of persecution in the third century, he was imprisoned near Rome on the Via Flaminia, where wild violets grew between stones, nooks, and crannies. Valentine picked heart-shaped violets and wrote with a stick on the heart-shaped leaves, "I love you," which he pushed out the prison bars. Passers-by received his "valentines." Variations of the story say he was imprisoned for performing marriage ceremonies for Christian couples who refused to worship the emperor.

The catacomb of St. Valentine was dug under Parioli Hill. Several hundred years after his death, a very large pilgrimage church was built over his tomb. Pilgrims came from all over Europe to worship in St. Valentine's Church and to pray at his tomb. During an earthquake the hill was sliced away, and the church was destroyed. The modern entrance to the catacomb is still at the base of Parioli Hill, close to Via Flaminia. Traveling from our apartment to the city center, we passed it frequently. One February 14th I drove by and saw that the wrought-iron fence had been unlocked and the door to the catacomb was open. A sign by the entrance indicated there would be a worship service at 11 a.m. I drove home, telephoned friends who lived in the north side of the city, and asked if they could come to St. Valentine's catacomb. Six of us met at the catacomb's entrance. We walked down the narrow, short, dark hallway to the empty tomb of the loving little priest whose name signifies love. We prayed, thanking God for a life that urged other people to share God's love. The body of St. Valentine is now entombed in a very small marble chapel in the Church of St. Praxedes in downtown Rome.

Father, thank you for the example of a simple man who embodied your love.

**In modern Italy only engaged couples
exchange gifts or greeting cards on February 14.**

St. Christopher

"The LORD is my strength and song, And He has become my salvation; He is my God, and I will praise Him; My father's God, and I will exalt Him."
Exodus 15:2

Often a St. Christopher medal is affixed to the dashboard or hung from a rearview mirror in Italian automobiles. Patron saint of travel, St. Christopher's responsibility is to protect travelers.

A great hulk of a pagan, Christopher heard of Christ and went to search for Him. A holy hermit told him, "Perhaps our Lord will show Himself to you if you fast and pray." "Ask me something easier," said Christopher. The hermit told him of a swift river, over which there was no bridge, that travelers feared. The hermit suggested Christopher live by the river and assist poor travelers across it. Perhaps the Lord would be pleased and show himself to Christopher.

So Christopher built a cabin by the riverbank. Using a tree trunk as a staff, he steadied himself in the rushing waters as he carried trusting travelers on his broad shoulders across the river. One night he was awakened by the voice of a child who cried, "Christopher! Take me across the river!" Christopher hurried out, staff in hand, and put the child on his shoulders and waded into the rushing water. The child seemed to get heavier and heavier until Christopher wondered if he would be able to endure the burden. With all his strength, he continued to walk, struggling to avoid dropping the child into the dangerous river.

Christopher told the child he felt he was carrying the whole world. The child replied, "Marvel not, Christopher, for you have borne upon your back the whole world and Him who created it. I am the Christ whom you serve in doing good deeds. As proof of my words, plant your staff near your cabin, and tomorrow it shall be covered with flowers and fruit." The huge man did what the little child told him, and the next day he saw his staff had grown into a beautiful date palm.

Holy God, help us serve you by helping those who cannot help themselves.

According to tradition, Christopher was martyred in Asia Minor during the third century.

St. Agnes

"But the very hairs of your head are all numbered.
Do not fear therefore; you are of more value than many sparrows."
Luke 12:7

In 1819, John Keats, English poet and Rome resident, wrote a dramatic poem set in Rome on January 20, the day before the feast of St. Agnes and traditionally the coldest night of the year.

In *The Eve of St. Agnes* Keats refers to several legends relating to this popular Roman saint. Agnes was born into a wealthy, pagan Roman family. When Agnes became a Christian, she resolved, as did many believers, to live a life of purity, consecrating her virginity to God. Her parents were furious over her profession of the Christian faith and tried to dissuade her from her vow. During the persecution of Christians by Diocletian in 304, she was denounced to the governor for refusing to offer sacrifice to Roman gods. Because she was only 13-years-old and from a prominent family, the governor tried to save her life by frightening her into submission.

Agnes was taken to a place where instruments of torture were displayed. When she showed no fear and refused to recant her Christian faith, she was sent to a brothel in the base of the Circus Agonalis. Ridiculed for her faith in Christ, she was stripped of her clothes. According to a Roman legend, her hair grew miraculously, quickly covering her body. Varying stories of her martyrdom agree that she retained her purity by her saintly bearing. When she was returned to the governor, he ordered her beheaded. One story says she was stabbed in the throat, another that she was martyred in the Circus. The death of this pure young woman had a profound effect on skeptical pagans. Agnes possessed spiritual peace they could not comprehend. In Piazza Navona, the Church of St. Agnes was built over the brothel where she was taken before her death. On Via Nomentana the Church of St. Agnes outside the Walls stands over the catacombs where she was buried.

Gracious Father, I know I am safe in your hands. Despite what might happen to me in this life, I know you will keep me eternally in your loving care.

St. Agnes is the patron saint of chastity, gardeners, girls, engaged couples, rape victims, and virgins.

St. Sylvester

"Shepherd the flock of God which is among you."
I Peter 5:2a

    "What are you your plans for San Silvestro?" is a common question one hears as soon as Christmas is past. Italians enjoy celebrating New Year's Eve, a holiday named for Sylvester, who was pope from 314 to 335.

    A very hospitable young person, one day Sylvester welcomed to his home a Christian named Timothy, whom no one was willing to receive for fear of being persecuted. After a year of preaching in Rome, Timothy was arrested, tried, and killed for his refusal to sacrifice to the pagan gods. Tarquin, the prefect of Rome, thought Timothy must have been very rich and demanded the dead man's money from his host. Tarquin threatened Sylvester with death if he did not give him Timothy's money. When Tarquin was convinced that Timothy had no wealth, he ordered Sylvester to sacrifice to the pagan gods, or he would be tortured on the following day. Sylvester said to Tarquin, "Thou fool, this very night thou thyself shall die and suffer the eternal torments of Hell, and shall be forced to acknowledge, willing or no, that the God whom we adore is the one true God!" Tarquin had Sylvester thrown into prison. That night while eating fish, a bone caught in Tarquin's throat, and he choked to death.

    Later, the people voted him as pope; as such Sylvester decreed that widows, orphans, and the poor should receive provisions from the church. He suggested fasting on Wednesday, Friday, and Saturday. He decreed that Thursday and Sunday should be days of worship. Although Sylvester was willing to die for his faith, it was not necessary because Constantine changed the political and religious climate of the empire. Legend says Sylvester baptized Emperor Constantine, cleansing him of leprosy. In 335 Sylvester died peacefully, giving three charges to his clergy: love each other, govern the churches with care, and guard the flock from the teeth of the wolves.

Loving God, may we seek to do your will every day of the year. Amen

As pope, Sylvester ordered the building of the first St. Peter's Basilica and the Basilica of St. John in Lateran.

St. Ambrose

*"Get wisdom! Get understanding!
Do not forget, nor turn away from the words of my mouth."*
Proverbs 4:5

Born in 339 in France, Ambrose was of an ancient Roman family, son of the Praetorian Prefect of Gaul. After his father's death, the family returned to Rome where Ambrose studied for a career in law and administrative duties. He lived in the stormy fourth century when barbarians flooded over the Alps and religious disputes caused factions among the people. The empire was tottering.

Ambrose was alarmed when he heard of the death of the bishop of Milan. Fearing a riot, he went to the basilica to keep order and advise the crowd to be moderate. He was so eloquent in his pleas, the people elected him bishop although he had never been baptized. Quickly he went through the various stages of instruction, baptism, and consecration as bishop. He resigned his legal position, gave away his property, and became a studious, concerned leader of the Christians of Milan.

When Emperor Theodosius' troops massacred 7,000 people in Thessalonica in reprisal for the murder of the governor and his officers, Ambrose denounced the emperor for his action and refused him the sacraments until he performed a public penance. The emperor obeyed the bishop, proving the power of bishop over emperor. It was a new day in the Roman Empire. Paganism in the empire was finally ended in 393 when an envoy was prevented from restoring it in Gaul. When Emperor Theodosius died a few months after his victory over the pagan forces, he died in the arms of Ambrose, who preached his funeral oration. As the Roman Empire was dying, Ambrose worked to establish Christianity in the West. He was a staunch defender of the independence of the church against the state. Ambrose died in 397 in Milan.

Most gracious God, help us to do those things you call us to do each day.

Ambrose is one of the four original Doctors of the Church—named in 1298—a designation to honor theologians of particular importance.

St. Jerome

*"All Scripture is given by inspiration of God, and is profitable for doctrine, for reproof,
for correction, for instruction in righteousness, that the man of God may be complete,
thoroughly equipped for every good work."*
II Timothy 3:16-17

An important saint for challenging times, Jerome was born Eusebius Hieronymus, in an alpine village of Dalmatia in 342. He studied in Rome where he was baptized at 18. He returned to his home and began living an ascetic life. He then went to Syria, where he became a monk. Though dedicated to the celibate life, he had strong sexual temptation that he learned to quell by intense study of Hebrew. He was ordained in Antioch, studied scripture in Constantinople, and returned to Rome in 382 where he was secretary to Pope Damasus I.

Damasus encouraged Jerome to translate the Bible as there was no uniform version of the Hebrew Old Testament and the Latin New Testament needed revision. His scholarship was unsurpassed in the early church. For 1,500 years Jerome's translation, known as the Vulgate Bible, has been the standard version for Roman Catholics.

In 385 after the death of Damasus, Jerome needed to leave Rome because he had made caustic remarks about some of his colleagues. He had given spiritual direction to Paula, a widow, and a group of pious women in Rome. Paula and some of these devout women followed Jerome to the Holy Land. They developed monastic communities of men and women in Bethlehem. Jerome devoted the remainder of his life to his work on Scripture. He lived the simple life of a hermit, helped the needy, and was greatly appreciated by his followers.

Nearly always a lion is depicted in paintings of the saint. The legend is that a lion with a sharp object in his paw limped to Jerome, who extracted the object and washed the wound. From then on the lion was his pet. The lion mourned for Jerome when the great scholar died in 420 in Bethlehem.

*Dear God, bless the efforts of dedicated translators so that people can read the
Good News of Jesus Christ in their own language.*

Jerome—along with St. Ambrose—is one of the original four Doctors
of the Church. Their statues stand in St. Peter's Basilica in Rome.

Pope Leo I

"Whoever confesses that Jesus is the Son of God, God abides in him, and he in God."
I John 4:15

Born about 400 in Tuscany, Leo was a Roman deacon who opposed heretics of the day. While in Gaul on a diplomatic mission for the imperial government, Leo was elected Bishop of Rome. He strengthened the church through a strong, central organization, based on the belief that the Bishop of Rome was the successor of Peter and therefore the leader of all bishops and all Christians in the world, giving him the title of Pope in the first use of the modern sense of the word. When Bishop Hilary of Arles challenged Leo, the powerful Leo had the bishop confined to his diocese by an imperial decree. Leo approved of and combined the forces of church and state to work together. He appropriated the authority and framework of the Roman Empire for the Roman Catholic Church, changing how "church" would be defined.

Though Leo knew no Greek and was not a profound scholar, he is known for the *Tome of Leo*, written for the Council of Chalcedon in 451. The Tome was accepted as a clear and basic statement of the person of Jesus Christ and was sent as a doctrinal letter to the patriarch of Constantinople. The Council of Chalcedon endorsed it with the famous words, "Peter has spoken through Leo."

A short excerpt from the Tome reveals Leo's faith: "Although he shared our humanity, and understood our weaknesses, he was not stained by our sin. He became human without detracting from the divine; and in this way he lifted humanity toward divinity. He made the invisible visible; he made the immortal mortal. This act of condescension was prompted by compassion for humanity's plight. The Son of God emptied himself of power, in order to reassert God's power over humanity." Pope Leo I died April 11, 461.

Merciful God, in our desire to be theologically correct, help us to be morally true, intellectually honest, and kind and loving with all of your children.

Leo was proclaimed a Doctor of the Church in 1574. Of the 13 popes named Leo, five have been canonized.

St. Benedict

"Draw near to God and He will draw near to you."
James 4:8a

Benedict, born about 480, was a simple man from the small town of Nursia. He went to Rome to study but was repelled by the decadence among laity and clergy. He withdrew to a cave near Subiaco, about 30 miles southeast of Rome. Other hermits came to join him. His twin sister, St. Scholastica, began a monastery in Subiaco for women.

About 525 Benedict left Subiaco and went to the ruined city of Cassino, located between Rome and Naples. Later he and his followers built a monastery on a hill above the town. Originally, the order was intended only for the laity. At Monte Cassino he expanded his plans for the reform of monasticism. Based on rules of other monastic leaders, he excluded austerities and the vow of poverty. Benedict worked and prayed at Monte Cassino until his death on March 21, 550. He is buried in the same tomb as his sister.

Monte Cassino Abbey, the largest of the Benedictine abbeys, was a very important cultural and religious center. In 1071 the magnificent abbey church was consecrated. It reached its greatest influence from 1058 to 1087 when Abbot Desiderius, later Pope Victor III, ruled. Manuscripts and paintings produced by the monks of Monte Cassino became famous throughout the world. In 1866 when the Kingdom of Italy dissolved many monasteries, Monte Cassino was declared a national monument. Its buildings housed a monastery, a school for laymen, and two seminaries. Its excellent collection of manuscripts is still housed in the library. During the invasion of Italy in World War II, German soldiers seized the hilltop monastery as a fortress. Bombs destroyed the ancient abbey. Through cooperation between Italy and the United States the monastery was rebuilt in 1952. The Benedictine monasteries in Subiaco and Cassino continue to be a source of delight to people interested in medieval Italy.

Lord, we know it is the Spirit who holds people together in their common faith. We thank you that it is the Spirit who initially confers on people the gift of faith, and brings them together to form a church. Thank you for your Holy Spirit, working in our lives. (Adapted from a prayer by St. Benedict.)

Sixteen popes have chosen the name Benedict, which means "blessed." Pope Benedict XVI was elected in 2005.

St. Francis of Assisi

"For whoever does the will of God is My brother and My sister and mother."
Mark 3:35

St. Francis—whom many believe is the most important Italian who ever lived—tried to be like Christ. He was even born in a stable, which can be seen on one of Assisi's narrow streets. Born to a French mother in the late 12th century, the baby was christened Giovanni but was always called *Francesco* or "Frenchman."

The town's leading playboy, he was friends with the nobility. During a war, Francis was captured and imprisoned. After this difficult experience, he found it impossible to settle back into his sheltered life. He went on a pilgrimage to Rome where he saw many beggars. In front of St. Peter's Basilica, he changed his appearance and begged for alms, elated to discover his dependence on God. He thought of Jesus who possessed nothing and depended on God's care completely.

When Francis returned to Assisi, he trusted God to provide his needs. He repaired the ruined Church of St. Damian below the city walls. While praying at the ancient church, he heard Christ speak to him from the old crucifix over the altar. Jesus had said to Peter, "You will build my church," and Francis heard those words as the Lord's command to himself. He picked up stones in the fields and repaired the walls. He begged for food and ministered to the poor, the sick, and the lepers.

Also known as "the little poor man," he preached the good news and had many followers who were discouraged by the secular life in Italy. Franciscans use the word "brother," not "monk," to describe themselves.

Two years before his death, Francis was praying at a retreat when he had a vision of a celestial creature. Immediately he received the gift of the stigmata. Until his death in 1226, he bore the marks of Christ's passion in his hands, feet, and side.

"All creatures of our God and King, Lift up your voice and with us sing. Alleluia!" (*from St. Francis' Canticle to the Sun*)

Francis repaired a little chapel known as St. Mary of the Angels. Reputed to have been built in 352, it became the center of the Franciscan movement.

St. Clare of Assisi

"A good name is to be chosen rather than great riches,
Loving favor rather than silver and gold."
Proverbs 22:1

Tourists gathered before the tomb of St. Clare. I waited in line to see her blackened body, stretched out in her glass-covered casket. The saint has been dead more than 700 years but her influence is still very much alive.

Before Clare's birth in 1194 in Assisi, her mother prayed and heard a voice saying to her, "Fear not; thou shalt safely bring forth a light that shall enlighten the whole world clearly." This blonde daughter of a wealthy family was baptized in the same church where St. Francis had been baptized 12 years earlier and where children of Assisi are still christened. Early she vowed her virginity to the Lord and began to wear a hair shirt under her clothes. After hearing Francis preach, she determined to leave her home and devote her life to prayer. One of Clare's cousins had joined Francis in his simple way of life. Aided by her aunt, Clare talked with Francis and told him of her spiritual aspirations. Dressed as a beggar, Clare begged for bread from door to door in Assisi, proving to Francis her desire to forsake all for Christ.

On Palm Sunday in 1212, Clare attended church at the cathedral with her family. That night after midnight, accompanied by her aunt, she went to where Francis and his followers welcomed her into the Franciscan Order. Francis cut Clare's hair. By torch light he led her to a convent of Benedictine nuns two miles away. In time Clare began an order of nuns at the restored Church of St. Damian. Thousands of women joined the order, and Clare became the abbess. By the time she had lived out her 59 years, more than 10,000 cloistered nuns were living in 60 convents in many nations. Today they are known as "the Poor Clares."

Lord, help us to receive and share your gifts of peace, love, and compassion.

Greatly admired, Clare was canonized in 1255,
only two years after her death.

St. Anthony of Padua

"The effective, fervent prayer of a righteous man avails much."
James 5:16b

The person for whom San Antonio, Texas, was named would probably have been surprised to learn of his adoration. One of Italy's most revered saints is not Italian at all. He was born of a noble family in Portugal in 1195. After becoming a Franciscan friar, he changed his name from Ferdinand to Anthony, possibly in honor of St. Anthony of Egypt who lived in the fourth century.

Anthony was a good student and a serious young man. When the remains of some Franciscans who were killed in Morocco were brought to Coimbra where he was a student, he was filled with a desire for martyrdom.

As a young friar, Anthony went to Morocco for missionary work and possible martyrdom but was forced by illness to return to Europe. He went to Assisi and had several assignments in Italy and France. A humble man, he was a fine scholar and teacher. Francis of Assisi appointed Anthony as lecturer in theology to the Franciscan Order, the first person to hold the position. In 1230 he was allowed to give himself fully to preaching in and near the northern Italian city of Padua. Anthony's preaching was directed against the vices of usury and avarice. He was successful in preaching to the heretics of Italy and France. During his life he was regarded as a miracle worker.

In sculpture and painting, St. Anthony is usually depicted with a book or lily, symbolizing his knowledge of scripture. His simple brown Franciscan robe is tied with a rope belt with three knots, representing the Trinity. He holds an infant Jesus. In most Italian churches that have an altar dedicated to St. Anthony, candles burn continually.

Anthony died in Padua in 1231 and was buried there.

Father, thank you for godly guidance from
those who study and teach your word.

St. Anthony is invoked for the return of lost property. He is the patron of the poor, the pregnant, and travelers.

St. Catherine of Siena

"If we live in the Spirit, let us also walk in the Spirit."
Galatians 5:25

Born in 1347 in the small city-state of Siena, Catherine's childhood play reflected her inner feelings. As she hopped on steps, she would say prayers. When Dominican monks passed the house, she ran into the street and kissed the ground where they had walked.

When Catherine was in her late teens, she told her parents of her childhood vow to remain a virgin and give her life to prayer. She joined the third order of the Dominicans, which allowed women to remain with their families and live a life of devotion at home. She prayed and meditated. She slept on boards with a rock as a pillow. According to contemporaries, she lived on nourishment from the Eucharist and asked for it to be served to her several times a week.

Catherine claimed to have had a "mystical marriage" with Christ, becoming his virgin bride. She said he taught her secrets of the faith and gave her abilities to read other peoples' minds and to foresee the future. Despite the fact she had no formal schooling, she could read. She claimed to have learned to write without instruction. She corresponded with friends, prelates, and princes. Feeling that God had given her the mandate to pray for and help the church, she wrote to the pope who was living in Avignon, France, and demanded he move the papacy back to Rome. Later, she traveled to Avignon and urged Pope Urban VI to return. He conceded to her persuading; the Great Schism had lasted 70 years. Catherine grieved over difficulties of Florence and Tuscany with the pope, and she prayed for the reconciliation of Catholics with the pope. Her final years were spent in Rome. Thin and emaciated, she continued to pray daily for the healing of the Roman Catholic Church.

Loving God, Help us to serve you with our hearts and with our minds.

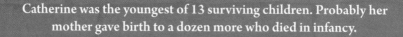

Catherine was the youngest of 13 surviving children. Probably her mother gave birth to a dozen more who died in infancy.

St. Frances of Rome

"Be faithful until death, and I will give you the crown of life."
Revelation 2:10b

Frances is said to be the favorite saint of the Roman people. She was born there in 1384 to a noble family. She desired to be a nun, but per her father's wishes married Lorenzo de' Ponziani. She was an exemplary wife and mother. She said, "A wife and a mother, when called upon, must quit her God at the altar, and find him in her household affairs." Frances and her sister-in-law, Vanozza, dedicated their lives to helping the poor by giving them food, clothing, and firewood. Instead of presuming on the prestige of her birth, Frances went to her own vineyard to collect firewood for the poor.

She founded The Oblates of St. Mary as an association of noble Roman ladies. With their husbands' support, the sisters give themselves to prayer and good works but without vows, strict enclosure, or giving up their property. After her husband's death, Frances entered the convent as a humble supplicant. She was happy to become a nun and was appointed the convent's mother superior. One day while working the vineyards of Porta Portese, they realized they had no food or water with them. Frances prayed, confessing her negligence in providing for her sisters. Almost immediately they saw a vine overhead bearing the exact number of clusters of grapes as there were hungry workers.

Frances left the convent to nurse her son who was ill and became ill herself. Her last words were, "The heavens open! The angels descend! The angel has finished his task. He stands before me. He beckons me to follow him." Frances died March 9, 1440. When her body was taken to Santa Maria Nuova to be interred, grieving mourners invoked her name in prayer and proclaimed her a saint. The church was renamed Santa Francesca Romana. It has one of the best organs in Rome.

Loving Father, protect us, guide us, welcome us into your eternal love.

Frances urged the people to call her "the poor woman of Trastevere."

St. Ignatius of Loyola

*"For the word of God is living and powerful, and sharper than any two-edged sword,
piercing even to the division of soul and spirit, and of joints and marrow,
and is a discerner of the thoughts and intents of the heart."*
Hebrews 4:12

Born about 1491 to a wealthy noble family, Ignatius chose a military career. In 1521 he was wounded; as he convalesced, he read biographies of the saints. At the Monastery of Montserrat, he confessed his sins, hung up his sword, and exchanged his princely clothes with a beggar. From there he went to Manresa where he prayed and engaged in mystical experiences that resulted in his writing *The Spiritual Exercises*.

In 1534 Ignatius worked out the idea of the Society of Jesus, a new religious order that would be at the service of the pope. Several of his companions decided on vows of poverty, chastity, a pilgrimage to Jerusalem—if possible—and a life of apostolic labors. While traveling to Rome to be ordained, he had the vision of La Storta, in which he was promised a good reception in the city. In 1540 Pope Paul III sanctioned the new religious order, and Ignatius became its first general. Members of the order—known as Jesuits— focused on education, a more frequent use of the sacraments, evangelization of pagans in the New World, and the fight against heresy. Some of the most outstanding scholars in the Catholic Church have been Jesuits. Ignatius died in 1556 and was canonized in 1622.

Not far from the Pantheon is the Church of Saint Ignatius, built between 1626 and 1685. Andrea Pozzo, a priest, painted the large frescoes on the flat ceiling of the church. His trompe-l'oeil represents the "Entry of St. Ignatiius into Paradise." To appreciate its full effect and artistic skill, one should stand on the small disk halfway up the nave. The eye is fooled, and the viewer has the sensation of looking beyond the flat ceiling into a limitless sky into which the spirit of St. Ignatius ascends toward Paradise.

*Teach us, good Lord, to serve Thee as Thou deservest: To give and not to count the cost; To fight and not to heed the wounds; To toil and not to seek for rest; To labor but ask for no reward, Save that of knowing that we do Thy will.
(Prayer for generosity by Ignatius)*

Today there are 3,730 Jesuit educational institutions throughout the world.

St. Teresa of Avila

"The LORD lifts up the humble; He casts the wicked down to the ground."
Psalm 147:6

An art-history professor needed help to find Bernini's statue *The Ecstasy of Santa Teresa*. Having only recently moved to Rome, I learned it is dramatically displayed in the Cornaro Chapel of the Church of Santa Maria della Vittoria. Bernini combined his knowledge of architecture, sculpture, and painting to create a marble masterpiece. In a recessed area at the front of the chapel, golden rays of light shine down on Teresa, a Spanish nun. An angel stands over her, pointing a golden arrow at her heart. Teresa's eyes are closed and she is focusing on the extreme pain and absolute joy and ecstasy of her experience.

Time seems to stand still as tourists observe the statue of this mystic who was born in 1515. She was not always spiritually sensitive. When Teresa was 16, her father sent her to a convent school, hoping the nuns could teach her discipline and purpose in life. He was not pleased when she decided to enter the local Carmelite Convent to become a nun. The original Carmelite vows of poverty, chastity, and obedience had changed. Life in the convent was typical of the times. In a relaxed atmosphere, the nuns lived in relative comfort, ate well, received guests, traveled, and retained servants. Through the years Teresa prayed and worked to bring discipline to the order. In 1562 in Avila she founded the Convent of St. Joseph. It was small, strict, and poor.

For the last 20 years of her life, Teresa traveled throughout Spain under difficult conditions, establishing convents and monasteries. Sometimes, in an intense state of spiritual joy, this mystic would levitate. Of one occasion she wrote, "I felt very distressed when I realized that my body was rising up, because I knew it would cause entertainment, and arouse talk. So I asked the sisters not to mention it to outsiders."

Loving Lord, we dedicate our bodies, minds, and souls to your glory.

In 1970 St. Teresa was named a Doctor of the Church for work in
the area of mystical theology and Christian spirituality.

Giordano Bruno

"He who justifies the wicked, and he who condemns the just,
Both of them alike are an abomination to the LORD."
Proverbs 17:15

Streets were made for strolling around *Campo dei Fiori*, the Field of Flowers, between Corso Vittorio Emmanuele and the Tiber River. On weekday mornings, a market is set up in the piazza. Housewives, restaurant chefs, and curious tourists walk around, find the best produce, bargain with vendors, and enjoy the hustle and bustle of a morning at the market. On Sundays the piazza is empty of vendors except for the flower stalls.

In the center of the piazza, a statue of Giordano Bruno stands watch over the market. Dressed in a monk's hooded robe, he stands as if in deep thought. Bruno was born at Nola in 1548 and joined the Dominican Order at Naples in 1562. A priest and scholar, he was convinced that the teachings of Copernicus about the shape of the earth and the movement of the planets around the sun were scientifically correct. Censured by religious authorities for his unorthodoxy, he fled from Naples in 1576.

For years Bruno was under constant suspicion. During visits to France, England, and Germany, he generated hostility in the academic community for his unconventional opinions. In his later years, some of his findings seemed to be in agreement with those of Galileo Galilei. Bruno's enthusiasm for nature led him to develop an extreme form of pantheistic immanentism, meaning that God was the efficient and final cause of everything: the beginning, middle, and end; the eternal and infinite. Wherever he went, he provoked the ire of his ecclesiastical enemies. Emissaries of the Inquisition arrested him and imprisoned him in Venice for six years and then in Rome for another seven. Charged with heresy, Bruno was burned at the stake on February 17, 1600, at Campo dei Fiori in the presence of a large crowd. Many other "heretics" died at this same site during the Inquisition. In the 19th century, a bronze statue was erected to honor his honest scholarship and intellectual honesty.

Thank you, Creator God, for creating man as an inquisitive being.

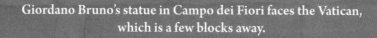

Giordano Bruno's statue in Campo dei Fiori faces the Vatican,
which is a few blocks away.

Pilgrimage to Rome

"And so we went toward Rome."
Acts 28:14b

Pilgrimages to holy places are undertaken by the faithful in every religious faith group. Traveling to Rome to see her holy places and the pope is a year-round activity for Roman Catholics. Many Roman Catholics travel to Rome for an Easter papal blessing or for blessings at a private or public papal audience.

One of the most famous pilgrimages to Rome was described by Hilaire Belloc in a diary he illustrated with pen and ink sketches. Belloc, a French intellectual, wrote many books in English. When he was in his hometown in Lorraine, he was surprised to see that the church of his childhood had been renovated. He noticed a statue of the Virgin Mary that was so exquisite, he decided at that moment to make a pilgrimage to Rome.

He determined to walk to Rome in as straight a line as possible. He walked up and down mountains, forded rivers, and went straight over the Alps and Apennines. He did not travel in the heat of the day but at night, early morning, and late afternoon. The long daylight of summer encouraged this schedule. Sometimes it was difficult to find food when he needed it. Some people were suspicious of the lone traveler who carried almost nothing with him but a bag for his bread and wine and a sketchpad.

The loneliness of the journey gave him time to think. He wrote his thoughts and sketched many scenes along the way. In traveling through France, western Switzerland, and Italy, he felt a spiritual bond with peasants along the way. He rejoiced in the Christian faith that had nurtured him and continued to give him encouragement. Belloc arrived on foot in Rome in time for the Feast of St. Peter and Paul on June 29, 1901.

*Lord, thank You for life's joyous journey and for
the challenge of reaching our goal.*

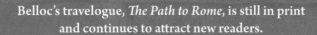

Belloc's travelogue, *The Path to Rome*, is still in print
and continues to attract new readers.

Padre Pio

"Then He said to Thomas, 'Reach your finger here, and look at My hands; and reach your
hand here, and put it into My side. Do not be unbelieving, but believing.'
And Thomas answered and said to Him, 'My Lord and my God!'"
John 20:27-28

A simple Capuchin monk lived a solitary life in southern Italy for many years. He was praying on September 20, 1918, when he received the stigmata, the visible marks of the crucifixion. Padre Pio lived for 50 years with unexplainable bleeding wounds on his hands and feet. For decades pictures of the bearded monk were everywhere in Italy. Every Friday Padre Pio presided at mass in a church near Foggia. In one Italian weekly magazine, an article told of how he prayed for Italy during World War II. Two American pilots were flying over southern Italy to drop bombs. Suddenly they saw a bearded man in a brown robe. He held his hands in a sign of peace and blessing. The pilots flew past and released the bombs into the sea.

The stigmata wounds do not become infected, and they resist ordinary treatment. They bleed mostly on Fridays and during Lent and Passion-tide. People who receive the stigmata are deeply religious, focused on the sufferings of Christ. Francis of Assisi is the first saint known to have received the stigmata. People who have the stigmata may also have other manifestations such as levitation and telepathic faculties. Padre Pio emitted a powerful floral scent and was said to be able to be in two places at once. People often asked him for healing. Pope John Paul II once asked Padre Pio to cure an ailing friend.

Bearing the stigmata is not enough for the Vatican to declare someone a saint. After Padre Pio's death in 1968, Catholics prayed to him for help in time of need. In 2000 in a hospital founded by the monk, a comatose boy was suddenly healed. The Vatican declared it a miracle. The boy was in the audience in St. Peter's Square on June 16, 2002, when Pope John Paul II declared that Padre Pio, born in 1887 as Francesco Forgione, was now a saint of the Roman Catholic Church.

Loving God, thank you for your abundant grace,
showered so generously on those who seek it.

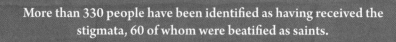

More than 330 people have been identified as having received the stigmata, 60 of whom were beatified as saints.

Death of a Pope

"The LORD shall preserve your going out and your coming in From this time forth, and even forevermore."
Psalm 121:8

During the summer of 1978, Pope Paul VI was ill. On Sunday evening, August 6, we were giving some visitors a last tour of Rome when we heard the announcement that Pope Paul VI had died at 9:40 p.m. Stunned by the news, we drove to St. Peter's Square to see what was happening. Many grieving people stood in the piazza. Groups of nuns prayed. International cameramen took pictures. NBC's cameraman focused on our small group. As we walked through the Bernini Colonnade and back to the car, we heard a bell tolling its mournful announcement of death.

When a pope dies, black gloom descends upon Rome. Funereal music is played on radio and television. Cultural programs are canceled. Vatican officials prepare for the funeral as well as for the Cardinal's Conclave that will elect a new pope. The conclave meets in the Sistine Chapel soon after the funeral, so it is closed to visitors until after the papal election. On Friday morning we went early to St. Peter's to view the body of the pope. By 7:30 a.m., a long line of people was waiting to enter. Swiss guards stood motionless on each side of the greenish-looking corpse. Newspaper articles said his body was decomposing rapidly because of the heat. (Embalming is not commonly practiced in Italy.)

On Saturday afternoon, I went to the Vatican for the funeral. Hundreds of chairs were set up in St. Peter's Square. Possibly 200,000 mourners stood in the sun or under the Bernini Colonnade. I joined a group of Polish tourists with seats in front of the stairs. The looming basilica provided a dramatic background for the ceremony and pageantry of the funeral. I recalled Luigi Barzini's description of St. Peter's as "the theater of God." I looked up at the statue of St. Paul and remembered the deep roots of the Christian faith.

*Lord, help us to leave a legacy of love and peace,
and of good deeds that help others.*

Pope Paul VI was the 280th pope.

Papal Audience

"Oh, clap your hands, all you peoples! Shout to God with the voice of triumph!"
Psalm 47:1

Piazza San Pietro was busy with the activities of hundreds of people on the spring morning when six of our church attended a papal audience. Already lines were forming to enter the hall. We waited for about 45 minutes, and then the lines began to move. After two checkpoints, finally our group walked into the beautiful marble hall.

Several attendants checked our tickets, and we went quickly to our assigned section. Before us was a tremendous, cavernous hall with thousands of seats. We were in a fenced-off area at the rear of the hall with standing space for many individuals and small groups.

We couldn't believe it: all that waiting—and no seats! For more than two hours we stood, watching thousands of empty seats fill with pilgrims. The crowd's excitement in anticipation of the pope's arrival could be felt. Finally, Pope John Paul II passed through the velvet curtain in the rear of the hall. People cheered, clapped, shook hands, and took pictures. Enthusiastic people shouted, "Here comes the pope!" No sporting event could have elicited more excitement and noise. People seemed electrified to be so close to the head of the world's largest Christian church.

Moving through the adoring crowd, the pope sat in a throne-like chair where he gave greetings and blessings in eight languages. The crowd sang a hymn and then began to leave. Our group was exhausted from standing still for five hours. As we left the hall, a French priest walking by said loudly, "I first came to Rome 50 years ago. I have been to Rome several times. I have served the church all my life, and now I have come to see the pope. They do not even have a chair for a 76-year-old priest." Exhausted, he walked with great effort. If anyone deserved a chair, he did.

Father, we are glad we need no appointment or ticket to come into your presence, but we thank you for religious traditions that fill us with joy and bring us together in praise.

Designed by Pier Luigi Nervi, the hall was built in 1971 to accommodate as many as 12,000 people.

Pope John XXIII

"Beloved, let us love one another, for love is of God; and everyone who loves is born of God and knows God. He who does not love does not know God, for God is love."
I John 4:7-8

Early Sunday morning in the summer of 1962, our family waited for a city bus. We heard a siren and saw motorcycles escorting a big sedan with flags flying. As the car turned, we saw Pope John XXIII, waving and smiling at us. He passed by in a moment, on his way to his summer palace at Castel Gandolfo. Smiling and goodwill were marks of his papacy.

This lovable pope, Angelo Giuseppe Roncalli, was born on November 25, 1881, in northern Italy. Some people called him a peasant, but he was well-educated. He studied in Bergamo and Rome and was ordained in 1904. He returned to Bergamo to be secretary to the bishop and to teach church history at a seminary. During World War I he served in the Italian army as a medical sergeant and a chaplain. During World War II he facilitated the rescue of Jews from Nazi-controlled Hungary. His international ministries brought him into contact with many different nationalities and religions. Through these responsibilities, he grew in his understanding of the need of differing people to understand each other.

Upon the death of Pope Pius XII, the College of Cardinals met to choose the next pope. Roncalli was elected pope on October 28, 1958. His chosen name indicated he was thinking in terms of reconciliation. John XXIII was the name of an antipope who ruled from France during the Great Schism. Since the 15th century, no pope had claimed the papal name of "John."

In 1959 John XXIII surprised the church and the world by calling the Second Vatican Council, which convened in 1962. The pope allowed great freedom for the council's studies and activities but reserved the right to approve its final decisions. Before the council could finish its work, John died in the Vatican on June 30, 1963. Pope John XXIII's loving attitude brought to the worldwide Christian community a spirit of cordial ecumenism.

We are grateful, our Father, for Christian leaders who live out your way of love on the world stage.

In Italy Pope John XXIII is remembered with the affectionate moniker *Il Papa Buono* or "The Good Pope."

Pope John Paul I

"Then our mouth was filled with laughter, And our tongue with singing. Then they said among the nations, 'The LORD has done great things for them.'"
Psalm 126:2

The last Sunday in August 1978 the newly proclaimed Pope John Paul I was to appear at noon on the balcony above the main entrance to St. Peter's Basilica. After morning worship, Dub and I took some of the youth from the church to witness this historic moment. At St. Peter's Square thousands of people were standing, awaiting his appearance. Popes always speak in the third person, but that morning the new pope broke with tradition and, laughing in disbelief, said, "Yesterday I was named pope." He laughed again, and the crowd clapped and showed their joy that Giovanni Luciani, a humble man from a small mountain village, had become the head of the largest religious institution in the world. He brought to the Vatican his simple lifestyle, disciplined study, and a desire to be a pastor to the people. His papal audiences had a spontaneity and warmth the thousands attending had never imagined possible. He began to make plans for sweeping reform in the church. Embarrassed by the riches of the Roman Catholic Church, he thought her wealth should be shared with the world's poor. Some church leaders were shocked at his evangelical zeal for the poor and unconverted. The 33 days of his papacy were probably filled with planning for future changes.

On September 29, Pope John Paul I was found dead in bed. Italians began to whisper that his death was suspicious. Strange facts came to light: the undertakers were called before a doctor was summoned; the pope's will and important papers listing his plans for that day had disappeared; some personal items had vanished. He had planned to remove people who had brought suspicion on the Vatican through international financial dealings. Clergy and Mafia stood to benefit from his death. Many have theorized the details of his mysterious death. There was no adequate explanation.

Father, help us to do the right thing, regardless of the cost.

Italians called Pope John Paul I *Papa Luciani*.

Pope John Paul II

*"For every high priest taken from among men is appointed
for men in things pertaining to God."*
Hebrews 5:1a

On October 16, 1978, the newly elected pope was presented to those waiting in St. Peter's Square. The first non-Italian to be elected in 455 years had the unpronounceable name of Karol Jozef Wojtyla. With a buoyant spirit, he greeted the enthusiastic crowd.

For the most part, people seemed pleased with the election of a compassionate person from Soviet-dominated Eastern Europe. John Paul II was an energetic 58 year old who spoke 3,000 times. In 1995 in Manila, he spoke to three million people, the largest audience in history. He canonized 456 saints.

Wojtyla was born in Poland on May 18, 1920. He attended public school and had close friends who were Communists, Catholics, and Jews. One of his closest Jewish friends, Jerzy Kluger, became an engineer in Rome and had the first private audience with newly elected John Paul. Through the years, the Kluger family enjoyed many evening meals with the Pontiff in his private apartment. Through his papacy, he tried to help bring peace to Israel. He wanted Jerusalem to be an international city where Jews, Christians, and Muslims could worship in peace.

In April 1982 a Turkish Muslim shot him in St. Peter's Square. Recovered from his wounds, he visited the man in his prison cell. On April 13, 1986, Pope John Paul II became the first pope to visit a synagogue and addressed Rome's Hebrew congregation. Chief Rabbi Toaff told a newspaper reporter, "You know the distance from the Vatican to this synagogue is very short—a few kilometers—but it took 2,000 years to cover it. And John Paul II did it."

The Polish pope encouraged Catholics in Poland and other Soviet-dominated countries to throw off their yoke of oppression. Communism crumbled. Partly through his efforts and those of other world leaders, the Berlin Wall came down in 1989. This pope's loving manner helped bring together people of differing faiths for dialogue.

Our Father in Heaven, bless us each day as we seek to live for you.

John Paul II chose his name to honor his predecessor, who had chosen his name to honor the legacies of Pope John XXIII and Pope Paul VI.

The Priest's Wife

"[The high priest] shall take a wife in her virginity."
Leviticus 21:13

On the subway in Rome, I sat facing a garrulous, chubby housewife who clutched her shopping basket and engaged everyone around her in conversation. She asked our nationality, what we were doing in Rome, did my husband work at the Embassy, was he a business man or a professor. "No? Then what does he do?" When I said that he was *un pastore*, a pastor, she was totally confused. In Italian, *pastore* means both shepherd and pastor and I did not look like a shepherd's wife. I tried to explain, and for lack of words said, "He is an evangelical pastor—like your priest." The horrified woman stood, pointed accusingly at me and announced as loudly as she could, "This woman is married to a priest, and this is their daughter!" Completely distraught, she got off at the next exit.

By the 1970s, priestly celibacy was of great concern to Catholics. Seizing on this interest, several plays and films focused on the issue. *The Priest's Wife*, starring Sophia Loren and Marcello Mastroianni was advertised on movie billboards all over Italy. Mastroianni, in a priest's black cassock, stood alongside an alluring Loren in front of St. Peter's. The film's plot was simple: a beautiful young girl was jilted by her lover; she turns to her priest for counseling after a suicide attempt. His compassion turns to passion, and he asks the Vatican for permission to marry. Permission is denied. Throughout the Catholic world, priests were asking the Vatican for permission to marry. Pope Paul VI was adamant that this Church rule would not change. The loneliness of the priest can be a heavy burden. On a crowded bus I overheard, "Do you think our priests will be able to marry?" The snappy, realistic reply came quickly, "No, not our priests, but their children will."

Thank you, Father, for life and all its joys and sorrows that teach us your way.

Priestly celibacy has been church law since the 11th century.

Pope Benedict XVI

"I can do all things through Christ who strengthens me."
Philippians 4:13

Joseph Ratzinger, a German cardinal, was Pope John Paul II's chief advisor on doctrine and his trusted confidant. "God's Rottweiler," as he is known, had helped the pope formulate important statements on theological, moral, and social issues as well as the relationship of the Vatican to Christian sects and other religious groups.

On April 19, 2005, just a few weeks after the death of the beloved John Paul II, Ratzinger stood on the balcony above the main entrance to St. Peter's Basilica and said to the crowds in the piazza, "Dear brothers and sisters, the cardinals have elected me, a simple humble worker in God's vineyard." There was joyous exuberance and applause from seminarians and others who wanted a strong pope. Disappointed Catholics responded in grudging silence.

Ratzinger was born April 16, 1927, in Marktt am Inn in Bavaria, Germany. At 12, he entered seminary. Two years later, he was forced to join Hitler Youth. His father, a policeman, was always at odds with Nazi officials. When Joseph was 16, he was drafted into the German military and assigned to an anti-aircraft gun crew. Before the war's end, he deserted. He was held briefly as a prisoner of war by American forces. With the war's end, he returned to seminary and was ordained to the priesthood in 1951. In 1981 Pope John Paul II appointed Ratzinger prefect of the Congregation for the Doctrine of the Faith, responsible for issues of orthodoxy within the Roman Catholic Church. In 2002 he was named dean of the College of Cardinals.

He chose the papal name of Benedict XVI. His name choice was influenced by the lives of St. Benedict of Nursia and Pope Benedict XV, who sought peace during and after World War I. Maybe the new pope will be conciliatory and peaceful as his namesakes.

Thank you, Father, for people who are willing to serve you in demanding places of leadership.

Joseph Ratzinger is the first German pope since 1523.

Section V
Buon Viaggio!

The Lake Country

"But Jesus withdrew with His disciples to the sea.
And a great multitude from Galilee followed Him."
Mark 3:7

Many tourists enter Italy by car, train, or plane from northern European cities. Entering from central Switzerland, one passes through an area that stretches from the foothills of the Alps to the plains of Lombardy. The area's glacier-formed lakes are celebrated for their beauty and calm. The largest lakes, from east to west, are Lake Maggiore, (northeast of Milan), Lake Lugano, Lake Como, and Lake Garda near Verona. An ingenious system of ferries and boats connects each lake's towns and islands. Some elegant homes, fantastic gardens, and charming towns can be visited by boat and by walking. Parking is limited. A few days in the lake region can be relaxing and recuperative after busy tourist schedules, standing in line, boarding buses or trains, or driving in fierce traffic.

Mountains protect Lake Maggiore's shores from alpine cold air. The result is a Mediterranean-type climate that encourages luxuriant growth. The resort town of Stresa has all the amenities for a delightful get-away in spring, summer, or autumn. In the 15th century the princely Borromeo family built several villas and gardens, now preserved as museums, on the Borromean Islands in Lake Maggiore. Winter-sport fans commute to nearby slopes for skiing. Lake Lugano extends into Switzerland where the town of Lugano has a distinctly Italian character

The city of Como on Lake Como is the busy provincial capital; it was conquered by the Romans in 196. Lake Como also boasts of Bellaggio with its splendid gardens and villas. Varenna, a charming village, is the choice of youthful hikers who don't mind the stairways that substitute for streets. Lake Garda borders on the Veneto region. It is the site of the town of Bardolino, noted for its red wine, and of Sirmione, an important spa whose waters are effective in curing respiratory diseases. The lakes are best enjoyed in sunny weather.

O Divine Creator, we are grateful for calm lakes, colorful flowers, fresh air,
sunshine, and good food shared with friends.

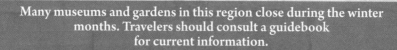

Many museums and gardens in this region close during the winter
months. Travelers should consult a guidebook
for current information.

Milan

"The rich man's wealth is his strong city."
Proverbs 10:15a

At the first sight of Milan, the tourist must remind himself he is in Italy and not in Germany or eastern France. *Milano*—pronounced with the accent on the second syllable—is in the middle of the Po River Valley. The largest river in Italy, the Po River makes it possible for the Province of Lombardy to have the most abundant crops and the heaviest fog south of the Alps. Through the centuries, barbaric hordes struggled over the Alps in search of productive land and sunshine. When mountain mists lifted, their eyes, full of surprise, looked down on the verdant valleys of the Po River. So many Lombards—Germanic people who first invaded Italy in the mid-sixth century—came and settled here that the area is named Lombardy for these tall, blue-eyed, industrious invaders. This most populous region of Italy is also the most productive, accounting for at least one-third of Italy's agricultural and industrial exports. The bustling city of Milan is at the heart of this farming area.

The University of Milan has long reflected the intellectual brilliance of northern Italy. During the Italian war of unification in the 19th century, Milan's intellectuals played an important role in helping Italy achieve independence from neighboring countries and from the papacy.

Milan's prosperity is worn ostentatiously and proudly. Museums, the LaScala Opera, hotels, public buildings, the gothic duomo, and lavish cemetery monuments reflect the city's great wealth and love of opulence. Her banking system early competed with that of Florence. Lombard Street—London's famous banking street—was named in recognition of the highly successful medieval Italian bankers.

Many foreign businessmen travel to Milan every spring for its *La Fiera Campionaria*, the international trade fair, which attracts buyers from all over the world. Textiles, the chemical-electrical industry, the automobile industry, ceramics, and the fashion industry are important in the life of Milan.

Father, thank you for interesting, prosperous cities that
support a pleasant way of life.

Milan is famous for its fashion houses, and the Galleria Vittorio Emanuele in the Piazza Duomo is reputed as the world's oldest shopping mall.

Venice

"He shall have dominion also from sea to sea."
Psalm 72:8a

Venice, or *Venezia* to natives, boggles the mind. As an Italian city, it is very young. It was not settled until the fourth century when mainland settlers fled to the northwest Adriatic islands to escape the barbarians. Early Venetians were fishermen and traders. An independent city-state ruled by nobles, Venice grew in power and wealth on her sheltered lagoons. Palaces, apartments, churches, and public buildings were built on large pylons sunk into the marshy ground. Within 400 years, Venetians established trade with cities on the Italian peninsula and with places as far away as Constantinople and North Africa.

Once Venice had 3,000 ships, 17,000 sailors, and 300 shipping firms. Now its main source of income is tourism. A wealth of art treasures asserts she is one of the world's cultural centers. Its location on the sea is now at risk. The rising seawaters constantly beat upon its structures, which are gradually sinking. Engineers from around the world try to find solutions for preserving this unique city.

When a person walks into St. Mark's Square, he is usually overwhelmed with its size but feels at home, having seen the famous piazza in many movies. The cavernous St. Mark's Basilica gives a feeling of mystery. The body of St. Mark, stolen from Egypt by Venetian sailors many centuries ago, is entombed there.

In July Venice celebrates the Roman Catholic Feast of the Redeemer, commemorating the end of the plague of 1575. Musicians perform nightly in lighted boats. In September the colorful gondola race and the Venice Film Festival attract enthusiastic crowds.

A tour of the city should include at least one glass-blowing factory. The island of Murano is famous for fine crystal and glassware. The island of Burano is famous for embroidery and lace. Shopping in Venice is an adventure as is dining. With a cuisine based on fish, Venetians enjoy long, leisurely mid-day meals and late, lingering evening meals.

*Father, thank you for beautiful places and fascinating people
who fill our lives with joy.*

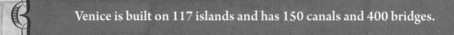

Venice is built on 117 islands and has 150 canals and 400 bridges.

Verona

"But the meek shall inherit the earth, And shall delight themselves
in the abundance of peace."
Psalm 37:11

Verona, one of the most ancient and beautiful Italian cities, is sometimes called "The Gateway to Italy." From Roman times it was one of the first settlements to be reached after crossing the Alps on the Brenner Pass. Through the years travel writers have remarked on this area where the River Adige, Lake Garda, the hills, and mountains provide pleasing landscapes. A flourishing city established long before Venice, it is located in the Province of Veneto. Everyone notices the city's beauty, made possible by lavish use of local pink marble, referred to as "peace blossom."

The city is rich in museums, important libraries, and heir of more Roman ruins than any Italian city except Rome. Verona has a smaller but better preserved Colosseum than Rome's, the third largest in the Roman world, used for entertainment for 2,000 years. Every summer the Arena of Verona hosts international opera with an impressive production of Aida and other works. Piazza Erbe's Roman Theater has been restored and has a museum and dramatic productions. Museums, gardens, churches, tombs of the Scaligeri family, and the medieval Castelvecchio tempt tourists to submit to the charms of the city.

Verona is attuned to learning. The University of Verona attracts some of Italy's brightest students. Mondadori, Italy's important publishing house, is located in Verona. Several medieval writers told the story of Julietta and Romeo, inspiring Shakespeare to write his immortal play. The tragic feud of the Montague and Capulet families reflects the realities of life in the 14th century. The romance of *Romeo and Juliet* attracts tourists to the balcony and the House of Juliet. Busloads of tourists visit the tomb.

The city and its province have international importance in industry, commerce, and agriculture. Every year Verona hosts the International Agricultural Show and the International Exhibition of Agricultural Machinery. The area produces wine, fruits, and marble for world markets.

Thank you, Father, for citizens who plan for the common good and help create
pleasant places to live.

Travel writer H. V. Morton wrote, "Of all the cities I had seen so far in Italy, Verona gave me the greatest pleasure. It was elegant, dignified, and beautiful."

Cremona

"Praise Him with the timbrel and dance; Praise Him with stringed instruments and flutes!"
Psalm 150:4

Cremona, a northern Italian city on the Po River, was founded by the Romans in 218 B.C. Between the 16th and 18th centuries, Cremona was famous for violins made by several generations of the Amati, Guarneri, and Stradivari families. One fall day, my husband and I had the privilege of touring the school of violin making. We arrived in the museum hall just as the attendant was putting the Stradivarius violin back in its climate-controlled glass case. Next to the Stradivarius, a Guarneri violin was displayed.

Andrea Amati, founder of the Cremona school of violinmakers, modeled his small violin with a high back and belly. His violins, varnished with an amber varnish, had a clear though weak tone. A grandson, Nicolo Amati, changed the design, using beautifully grained wood and arching the backs and bellies of the instruments. He was the last of the family involved in violin making.

Andrea Guarneri learned violin making in the workshop of Nicolo Amati. His sons learned the trade, and their modified instruments are also highly prized. Nicolo Paganini, among other violinists, prized the rich tone of his Guarneri.

Antonio Stradivari also studied violin making with Nicolo Amati and perfected the art of making violins, violas, and cellos by making some changes in the proportions. Musicians have tried to discover the secret of the beautiful sound of his instruments and are undecided if it is the varnish, the type of wood, or the design that gives them such a glorious sound. They are the most desired in the world. Several hundred of his violins survive. Fewer violas and cellos are known to exist. His finest instruments were made between 1700 and 1725. Stradivari, the father of 11 children, lived to be 90. Modern musicians use the Latinized version of his name, *Stradivarius*, in reference to the violinmaker.

Father, thank you for music, musicians, and makers of instruments.

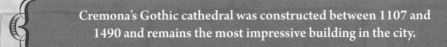

Cremona's Gothic cathedral was constructed between 1107 and 1490 and remains the most impressive building in the city.

Turin

"For the LORD your God has blessed you in all the work of your hand."
Deuteronomy 2:7a

"They are born mechanics," it is said of the people of Turin. This city, which Italians all *Torino*, is the capital of Italian engineering and the home of the Italian motor industry. The city's symbol is a strong, tenacious bull or toro. Torino, the little bull, lives up to its name.

Laid out in a grid beside the Po River, it is ringed by the distant Maritime Alps. Good views of the city are enjoyed from Mole Antoneliana, a fortress built in the 19th century. Close to the French border, Turin is the most French of Italian cities. French influence can be heard in the dialect of the farmers, tasted in the cuisine, and seen in the architecture. This lively, prosperous town has wide, arcaded avenues and 166 spacious piazzas. The city's public transportation system was improved for the 2006 Winter Olympics.

Turin is largely the legacy of the House of Savoy, the oldest monarchy in Europe until its removal from power in 1946. Kings Carlo Alberto and Victor Emmanuel II figured in the struggle for Italian unification during the 19th century. In the Palace of the Academy of Science are housed a museum of antiquities, an Egyptian museum, and two art galleries. Also prized are museums of ancient art, modern art, a film museum, and a car museum.

One of the city's religious treasures is the Sacred Shroud of Turin. Reputed to be the linen shroud in which the crucified Christ was wrapped, this long piece of cloth bears the image of the person who had been wrapped in it. Many prelates and scientists have examined the shroud to determine its age. Some authorities say it is authentic; others doubt its provenance. It had long been the property of the House of Savoy and was kept in the Chapel of the Holy Shroud in St. John's Cathedral. In 1983 King Umberto died, leaving this relic to the Vatican. The shroud remains in Turin.

Father, thank you for peaceful cities where people work harmoniously together.

In the 19th century, St. John Bosco—founder of the Salesian Order—began his compassionate work with abandoned children, training them in a trade.

Genoa

"There are three things which are too wonderful for me, Yes, four which I do not understand: The way of an eagle in the air, The way of a serpent on a rock, The way of a ship in the midst of the sea, And the way of a man with a virgin."
Proverbs 30:18-19

The greatest seaport in Italy, Genoa spreads out its impressive buildings and palaces in a mountain amphitheater on the Gulf of Genoa on the Tyrrhenian Sea. From its beginnings, Genoa has been tied to the sea.

Genoa was French under the First Empire and was besieged by the Austrians. It became a part of Italy during the unification of Italy. Giuseppe Mazzini, native of Genoa, was one of the architects of the new Italy. The industrial revolution changed Genoa, which developed steelworks and a railway hub. Because of the wealth brought to Genoa by its shipping businesses, for centuries there were fabulously wealthy families who built and decorated great palaces for themselves. Some of the palaces are now museums with much art. But Genoa declined after World War II.

In 1985 the European Union planned to focus on a different European city each year. Genoa's special year as a European "capital of culture" was inaugurated on New Year's Day 2004. Planned were more than 200 events dedicated to art, music, literature, science, history, sports, and to children. Ninety conferences and international conventions were scheduled. To prepare for the year, extensive renovation of museums and palaces was accomplished. A new street lighting system was installed. In 1992, as part of the celebration of the 500th anniversary of Columbus' discovery of the New World, Europe's largest aquarium was built. It harmonizes with two museums dedicated to the sea and navigation.

Genoa is worth seeing for its own self and is more than a place where travelers debark from a cruise or change trains on a trip to somewhere else. Sample many kinds of seafood while in Genoa. Sights to see include the Cathedral of St. Lawrence and the statue o Genoa's most-famous native son, Christopher Columbus.

Father, thank you for courageous sailors whose hard work makes life easier for the rest of us.

Romans say the Genovese are the thriftiest people in Italy.
Instead of saying, "Let's go Dutch," Italians say,
Andiamo alla genovese—each person pays his own bill.

Cinque Terre

"But those who wait on the LORD Shall renew their strength; They shall mount up with wings like eagles, They shall run and not be weary, They shall walk and not faint."
Isaiah 40:31

Cinque Terre, or the "five lands," is a group of five fishing villages on the Italian Riviera. Passed in fleeting moments on the train that connects Genoa and Rome, the beautiful hiking trails that connect them have become one of the favorite destinations for hikers and young tourists. These isolated, medieval towns that are reached best on foot are situated on rocky cliffs. Vineyards run down to the sparkling, blue Tyrrhenian Sea.

The 15-kilometer path that connects the five villages follows the seacoast and can be walked in four or five hours, or in several days, depending on the time and desire of the hiker. Accommodations can be found in any one of the five towns, and a local train connects the villages for those not wishing to make the strenuous-at-points hike. There is also a ferry service for those wanting a different perspective of the rugged terrain. The region is known for its pesto and focaccia.

Experienced hikers recommend beginning the walk at the southernmost town, Riomaggiore, which is north of the city of La Spezia. Between Riomaggiore and Manarola there is the Via dell'Amore, or "The Way of Love," where for years young lovers found secluded places for *amore*. The next town is Corniglia, farthest from the shore. Then comes the Guvano, a nudist beach, on the coast below the town of Vernazza. The last of the five towns, Monterosso al Mare, has the only sandy beach in this part of the Italian Riviera.

Cinque Terre is now a national park and requires a nominal fee to hike on the well-maintained trails. The fantastic views, sea air, dramatic scenes, and an exhilarating touch with nature await the energetic tourist.

For the beauties of sky and sea, of land and growing things,
we give you thanks, O Lord.

Monterosso has the most traditional tourist attractions of the five cities with its beach, a castle, and a 17th-century monastery.

Bologna

Set in the rolling hills and farmlands of Emilia-Romagna, Bologna is known for its pork products—the same-named inexpensive sandwich meat came to America with Italian immigrants—cheeses, and meaty pastas. Bologna hosts an International Food Fair in late May and early June. In September, its splendid leather goods and its fashions are featured at the Shoe Fair and at the Fashion Show. A city of art, it is also an important industrial and commercial center. Bologna has an air of affluence and well-being.

Founded by Etruscans, the original site was named Felsina. Gauls, Romans, papal forces, and the French conquered the city through the centuries. It became a part of the kingdom of Italy in 1861. During World War II, it was heavily bombed by the Allies and then by retreating Germans in 1945.

Citizens of Bologna enjoy its picture gallery, archeological museum, palaces and piazzas, and some beautiful old churches. After becoming bishop of Bologna about 432, St. Petronius erected St. Stephen's Church. St. Stephen's is near the Church of the Holy Sepulchre through which one can enter the Court of Pilate, which is named for a basin attributed to be the one in which the Roman governor Pilate washed his hands before the crucifixion of Christ. The Basilica of St. Petronius, a fine Gothic structure begun in 1390, was the site of the coronation by the pope of Charles V as Emperor of the Holy Roman Empire.

A characteristic of this city is that it is brick, not stone. In the town center Bologna has covered sidewalks and leaning towers that give beauty and interest. A guidebook recommends four hours for a fast look. That's a "bunch of baloney" because this ancient city with its Old World atmosphere deserves plenty of time for the enjoyment of its pleasures.

*Loving Father, thank you for good food and the fellowship
we enjoy when we dine with friends.*

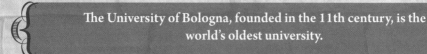

The University of Bologna, founded in the 11th century, is the world's oldest university.

Ravenna

"Jesus said to him, 'Have I been with you so long, and yet you have not known Me, Philip? He who has seen Me has seen the Father; so how can you say, "Show us the Father"?'"

John 14:9

Ravenna, the capital of Ravenna Province, is in the Emilia-Romagna Region near the Adriatic. A center for processing and marketing agricultural products of the province, Ravenna also has large petro-chemical industries and a cement factory. The Corsini Canal connects Ravenna to the sea.

In the first century Emperor Augustus built a canal connecting Ravenna with the Po River and enlarged its port of Classis. The Roman fleet in the northern Adriatic was based there. When the Visigoths threatened to invade northern Italy in 402, Roman Emperor Flavius Honorius moved to Ravenna from what is now Milan. Ravenna was the chief imperial residence until 476 when Odoacer, a German barbarian ruler, captured it. Almost 20 years later Theodoric conquered Ravenna and made it his capital. In 540 Belisarius, a Byzantine general, captured Ravenna and made it the seat of the Byzantine representatives who ruled Italy. Byzantine art was stamped forever on the principal buildings of the city. Ravenna was attacked in later centuries by the Lombards and by the Franks. It was given to the papacy, came under Venetian control, reverted to the papacy, and finally in 1861 became a part of the Kingdom of Italy.

Ravenna is famous for its fifth- and seventh-century buildings and for the colorful mosaics that decorate the interiors. Art historians come from all over the world to study them. The Church of San Vitale, consecrated in 547, is one of the best preserved. The Tomb of Galla Placida also has exquisite mosaics.

After Dante Alighieri was banished by his native city of Florence, he was welcomed by Ravenna where he lived until he died and was buried there in 1321. In 1483 the people built a marble temple-tomb to honor this famous Italian writer. On the funeral urn containing his ashes are the words of a Latin epitaph, and these added words: "Here in this urn lies Dante, exiled from his native land, born to Florence, an unloving mother."

We are grateful, our Father, for treasures from the past and achievements of your faithful followers.

Dante is buried in a tomb annexed at St. Francis' Basilica.

Florence

*"Unless the LORD builds a house, the work of the builders is wasted.
Unless the LORD protects a city, guarding it with sentries will do no good."*
Psalm 127:1 (NLT)

Everyone who visits Italy should see Florence. Inch for inch it may have more important artistic and historical items than any other city in the world.

Florence—or *Firenze*, as it known to the Italians—is located on the Arno River in central Italy, about 60 miles inland from the Ligurian Sea. In a valley between beautiful hills, the city rises only 164 feet above sea level. In the summer it is the hottest city in Italy, and often in winter its temperatures register as the coldest. Built upon an old Etruscan settlement dating to 1000 B. C., in the first century A.D. the village was developed into a colony for Caesar's veterans. It was named Florentia so that the new city might grow and "flourish." This capital of the province of Florence and of the region of Tuscany is known as "City of Flowers."

Piazza della Signoria, once the center of political activity, is a major tourist attraction. In front of the Palazzo Vecchio stands a copy of Michelangelo's *David*, a strong Renaissance symbol of the rising might of Florence under Medici rule. The original *David* is found in the Academia along with some of Michelangelo's other sculptures. The Loggia dei Lanzi contains some of the most famous statues ever carved. First-time visitors to the city will recognize Brunelleschi's *duomo* with Giotto's bell tower visible behind it.

During the Renaissance, a covered bridge was built to connect the residential Pitti Palace with the office building, or *Uffizi*, of the city. This bridge is known as *Ponte Vecchio*, which translates literally to mean "old bridge." Both the Uffizi and Pitti Palace now are world-famous art galleries.

A city of great museums, Florence is also a shopper's paradise, offering fashionable clothing, leather goods, jewelry, and art. Legend says shoppers at the Mercato Nuovo should rub the bronze boar's nose—known as *Il Porcellino* to locals—to ensure they return to this amazing city.

Father, Creator, thank you for inspiring your children to be artistically creative.

**Eighty-five percent of the gold chains sold in the world
are made in or near Florence.**

Pisa

"For You have been a shelter for me, A strong tower from the enemy."
Psalm 61:3

Tradition says that Simon Peter, en route to Rome, landed at the thriving port of Pisa, known today as San Piero a Grado. Once a strong maritime power, the Arno River has since silted up the harbor, and Pisa is now six miles from the sea.

Nowhere on earth is there a more harmonious group of religious buildings. Arrive early at the Piazza dei Miracoli before thousands of other eager tourists spoil your view, which is best seen by entering through the Porta Nuova. A large cathedral, or *duomo*, is the center of the grouping. In front of it is the round baptistery. To the extreme right is the Campo Santo, a cemetery that contains soil brought by the Crusaders from Jerusalem. Behind the cathedral, one can see the most famous tower in the world.

The Duomo was built in the 11th and 12th centuries. Its architecture—known as Pisan Romanesque and characterized by black and white marble stripes, arches, columns, mosaics, and colored marbles—was copied by many Tuscan cities.

The architecture is repeated in the baptistery and tower. Usually a guide will sing a few notes in the baptistery so spectators can hear the echo as the music travels around the curved wall.

The Bell Tower—or The Leaning Tower of Pisa—was begun in 1173 by Bonnano Pisano. Because of the alluvial subsoil, it began to tilt almost immediately and now leans almost 14 feet out of true at the top. It was closed to tourists in 1990 as experts tried to secure the tower without taking the characteristic lean out of it; it reopened to visitors in late 2001. Climbing around and around to the top is a dizzying, unforgettable experience.

Pisa, home of the University of Pisa, is an important business and industrial center. The Festival of Pisa's patron saint, St. Ranieri, is celebrated on the banks of the river on June 16. The Leaning Tower is celebrated every day.

Thank you, Father, for communities that value learning, tradition, and faith.

Galileo Galilei, a native Pisan, formulated a theory of the movement of the pendulum by studying the chandelier in the Duomo.

Perugia

"The lines have fallen to me in pleasant places; Yes, I have a good inheritance."
Psalm 16:6

The heady aroma of simmering dark chocolate is wafted uphill by currents of air from the Tiber Valley below. The Perugina factory produces delicious chocolate daily.

At least 3,500 years ago Etruscans moved to this safe hilltop from the eastern Mediterranean. Octavian (later Caesar Augustus) conquered Perugia in his effort to defeat Mark Antony. On the ancient Etruscan city gate, Octavian carved his name and victory. In the same part of the city is the University of Perugia, the fifth oldest university in the world.

The rule of the Roman Empire collapsed in the fifth century, but Perugia remained an important city in the region. Seeing it today, one can imagine what must have been its grandeur as its agriculture, artisanship, and religious and legal authority dominated life in Umbria. Medieval Perugia was Guelph, faithful to the pope and in opposition to the Ghibellines, who favored the aristocracy. Modern Perugia strives to maintain the medieval character of the city, and the ancient buildings and site are maintained in excellent condition. One evening our family attended a symphony in Perugia's main piazza. I looked around at the towers and the gothic cathedral and heard water splashing in the most beautiful medieval fountain in Italy. It was a clear night and a gentle breeze was blowing up from the valley. As the orchestra played its romantic themes, Peggy tugged on my arm and asked, "Mother, where are the fairies?" The setting looked like a page from a book of fairy tales.

Local citizens conduct big business with chocolate, flour, pasta, baked goods, agricultural products, and clothing. Perugia has much to offer to the tourist who comes to see the works of native artists Perugino, Pinturicchio, and Raphael. People can walk to the city garden for a great view of Assisi, 20 kilometers away, and to the Cathedral of St. Lawrence that protects the wedding ring of the Virgin Mary.

We are grateful, our Father, for cities where people value the past and live responsibly in the present.

Perugia is the hilltop provincial capital of Umbria.

Assisi

"The LORD bless you and keep you; The LORD make His face shine upon you, And be gracious to you; The LORD lift up His countenance upon you, And give you peace."
Numbers 6:24-26

Assisi has been standing a long time. An old legend asserts that Dardanus founded the city 865 years before Rome. He dedicated the town's temple to Minerva as an act of thanksgiving. Later, the Romans restored the temple, which still stands in the center of Assisi in Piazza del Comune. Now a church, the classical building is a reminder of the extent of Roman rule.

A person can stay economically in Assisi for many days. Several monasteries, guesthouses, and study centers offer room and board. An extended visit provides time to see the Cathedral of San Rufino, named for the martyr who brought Christianity to Assisi. The Basilica of Santa Chiara has the remains of St. Clare, founder of the female order of Franciscans. The Basilica of San Francesco houses the principal monastery of the followers of St. Francis. The serious tourist drives into the hills to see the *l'Eremo*, the Hermitage where Francis and his followers meditated in caves in a peaceful retreat on Mount Subasio above the city. A favorite picnic spot is the Rocca Maggiore, the 12th century castle that once defended Assisi.

Tourist buses drive to the three-level Basilica of St. Francis. Badly damaged by an earthquake in 1997, the church has been repaired. In the upper sanctuary, priceless frescoes by Giotto, *The Life of St. Francis*, have been restored. In the sanctuary's middle level are a wonderful old choir stall and many chapels. A frescoed portrait of Francis by Cimabue is thought to be an accurate likeness. When the choir sings Gregorian chants, the music echoes in the sanctuary. On the lower level of the basilica is the tomb of Francis and several of his followers. Often a pilgrimage group has mass or says the rosary at his tomb, the greatest treasure of the city and of the Franciscan order.

Father, thank you for saints of all ages. Help us to be instruments of your peace in our communities.

When St. Francis neared death, he gave his blessing to Assisi: "God bless thee, holy city; because through thee many souls will be saved, and in thee many servants of God will inhabit, and many of thy sons will be elected to the kingdom of eternal life."

Elba

"For the LORD your God is bringing you into a good land …
a land whose stones are iron and out of whose hills you can dig copper."
Deuteronomy 8:7a, 9b

Many Europeans camp and enjoy relaxed life on the island of Elba's beaches. Boats from Livorno and Marino di Campo connect Tuscany with Elba, which is about six miles from the mainland. For thousands of years, because of her strategic position in the Mediterranean, Elba has been fought over by Italians, French, Spanish, English, Tunisians, and other North Africans.

Early settlers discovered iron in its rocky soil and had a thriving business of supplying iron to peoples in the Mediterranean. Besides iron, it is rich in other stones and minerals. Columns for the Pantheon in Rome and stones for buildings in Pisa were quarried here. Before World War II the smelting of iron was one of the main sources of income.

The island's agriculture focuses on grape production. Fishing is another industry that is native to the area. Tourism in the last few decades has greatly increased

In 1801 Elba was ceded by the King of Naples to the French. Napoleon's sister Elisa Bonaparte was ruler, beginning in 1809. From May 3, 1814, to February 26, 1815, Napoleon was in exile on Elba. Sovereign of the island, he was adored by his subjects. A town house where he and his sister Paolina lived after the Treaty of Fontainebleau in 1814 is now a museum of great historical value. It contains priceless pictures, prints, proclamations, and Napoleon's book collection. At San Martino, a country home was acquired for Napoleon through the sale of some of Paolina's diamonds. The house is now a very impressive museum. After Napoleon's escape from Elba and his defeat by Wellington at Waterloo, Elba was reunited to the Grand Duchy of Tuscany until its union with Italy in 1860. Since World War II Elba has had a period of peace and prosperity. She enjoys her place in the sun and the good life of pleasant days and balmy nights.

Maker of heaven and earth, thank you for beautiful islands and sunny beaches,
for a harmonious blend of sea, sky, and fruitful land.

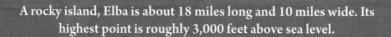

A rocky island, Elba is about 18 miles long and 10 miles wide. Its highest point is roughly 3,000 feet above sea level.

Viterbo

"To everything there is a season, A time for every purpose under heaven."
Ecclesiastes 3:1

An April day is perfect for a trip to the Italian countryside. Fruit trees are in bloom. The landscape is alive with new spring green. People bask in the sun. From Rome one can travel in any direction and have a delightful day of sightseeing. Drive north of Rome on the Via Cassia to Viterbo, a city of almost 50,000 people. For 2,000 years people have lived on this hill which changed from being an Etruscan city-state to a Roman colony. Viterbo was the seat of the papacy during a period of dissidence between the popes and the city of Rome, and it was the seat of the first papal conclave. Viterbo venerates St. Rose, who died in 1252 at the age of 17. Miracles were attributed to her, and she was canonized as a saint. Her tomb is in the Church of Santa Rosa.

Every nook and cranny of the city seems to echo historic events. It is easy to imagine life through the centuries. Narrow streets encourage pedestrian traffic. Major tourist sites are the Cathedral of San Lorenzo, beautiful fountains, the papal palace, and the Monastery of St. Mary of Truth. The monastery's Gothic cloisters house the Municipal Museum with its Etruscan collections from the area. After the hectic pace of modern Rome, a few hours in Viterbo help a person relax in the atmosphere of a well-maintained medieval city. Good restaurants abound. Thermal baths are available.

Delightful walks to the ruins of Ferentum, Villa Lante, and the Cistercian Abbey of San Martino al Cimino may be enjoyed. By car one can travel on narrow, winding roads to old churches, like the Church of the Madonna of the Oak, four miles away. Lake Vico is less than an hour by car. This small lake was the crater of a once active volcano.

Father, when we see how Italians treasure the past, we are grateful we can gain insight from people who lived long ago.

Every year on the night of September 3, 80 men carry the *macchina di Santa Rosa* in a procession. The huge wooden structure, lighted with lanterns, honors the saint.

Seven Hills

"In all your ways acknowledge Him, And He shall direct your paths."
Proverbs 3:6

Most tourists know that seven hills make up Rome, but when people try to name them, there is some disagreement.

The Capitoline, the smallest, but the most famous of the hills, was the ancient city's stronghold and religious center. It was accessible only from the southeast side, where the Roman Forum is located. Under an oak tree on the Capitoline Hill, early Romans sacrificed animals to Jupiter. Every tourist needs to walk up the *cordonata*, the staircase designed by Michelangelo for the visit of Emperor Charles V. The bronze equestrian statue of Marcus Aurelius stands in front of the Campidoglio and between the Campidoglio Museum and the Palazzo dei Conservatori. From the modern back side of the hill, one can enjoy a full view of the Forum.

The Palatine Hill, above the Forum, was encircled with a plow by Romulus. It was the original fortress for the Romans. From the base of the hill, there was easy access across the Tiber River. The nobility, and later the emperors, built fine homes on the hill. Because of descriptions by Ovid, it is possible to name the homes and public buildings that still stand on its summit. The House of Livia, the wife of Augustus Caesar, allows one to see how very well some ancient Romans lived. The Palatine Hill was once known as "the Palace of the Monarchy of the Earth." The word "palace" is derived from *palatine*.

The Esquiline Hill above the Forum and Colosseum includes ruins of the Golden House of Nero, Baths of Trajan, and Market of Trajan. The area has been leveled off many times for construction projects. It is best recognized by pedestrians as a formidable hill when they walk up Monte Oppio from the Forum or Colosseum to see what is left of the gigantic palace of Nero that sprawled over hills and valley.

Father, thank you for hills and mountains that lift our eyes
and thoughts to the heavens and to you.

The best views of Rome are from hills outside the old city walls.

Seven Hills, Part II

"But the land which you cross over to possess is a land of hills and valleys, which drinks water from the rain of heaven."
Deuteronomy 11:11

The Quirinal Hill was originally the stronghold of the Sabines. It is the site of the Quirinal Palace, the residence of the President of Italy. Begun in 1574 by Pope Gregory XIII, the palace was built to be a summer residence for the popes. In 1870, after the unification of Italy, the building became the property of the Italian government, and popes lived in the Vatican Palace. When foreign dignitaries make state visits to Italy, they are greeted at the Quirinal. On the piazza in front of the palace is a sculptural masterpiece of Castor and Pollux and their steeds. Because of them, the Quirinal Hill is sometimes known as Monte Cavallo, the "Horse Mountain."

The Spanish Steps march up toward the Church of Trinita dei Monti. At the top of the Steps, turn left to continue walking up the Pincian Hill past the Villa Medici to the top of the hill. From Piazzale Napoleone I Romans enjoy a dramatic view of the city. Many people come for the satisfying experience of being with others in an incredibly beautiful place. The Pincian Hill—called *Il Pincio* by the locals—is on the north end of the large Borghese Park.

The Caelian Hill, near the Colosseum, seems to be set in the Middle Ages. Ancient churches, monasteries, and Villa Celimontana Park can be enjoyed here. The Church of St. Stephen in the Round is an unusual octagonal church, decorated with disturbing frescoes of Roman martyrs. The Church of Santa Maria in Dominica was built over the house of Santa Cyriaca, a pious maiden of the third century.

The Aventine Hill, located south of the Circus Maximus, is quite removed from the rush of the city. Several ancient churches, the Villa of the Knights of Malta, and beautiful private villas are located here. Some of the best views of St. Peter's Basilica can be enjoyed from the hill.

Thank you, Father, for Rome, blessed by nature and historic events.

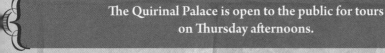

The Quirinal Palace is open to the public for tours
on Thursday afternoons.

The Pantheon

"In the beginning God created the heavens and the earth."
Genesis 1:1

On every modern tourist's must-see list, even during imperial times, the Pantheon was considered one of the marvels of the ancient world. The Pantheon was built in 27 B.C. to honor seven Roman planetary gods, particularly Mars and Venus. The earrings on the statue of Venus were said to have been halves of a giant pearl that had belonged to Cleopatra. Each god or goddess stood in a niche. The impressive temple became a symbol of the emperor's supremacy. As its name indicates, it was for the worship, *theon*, of all, *pan*, the gods.

Emperor Hadrian reconstructed the temple during his reign from 110 to 125. In 399 the temple was closed as a place of pagan worship, and it is fortunate that it was not destroyed. In 608 Byzantine Emperor Phocas, the overlord of Rome, gave the Pantheon to Pope Boniface IV. Boniface renamed and dedicated it as a Christian church to honor "St. Mary and all the saints and martyrs." Twenty-eight cartloads of martyrs' remains were brought from the Catacombs and re-interred in the Pantheon, a gesture of the triumph of Christianity over paganism.

Structurally, the Pantheon is much as it was during the reign of Hadrian. The floor was relaid in precious marbles during the pontificate of Pius IX in 1873. The diameter of the building is equal to the height—143 feet. The dome is 43.30 meters in diameter, the largest in the world. The open aperture in the center of the dome is 28 feet in diameter. Through the opening one can see moving clouds, blue or gray skies, or feel the splash of rain. There is no other building like it in the world and few as old.

God of all the earth, we cannot imagine the immensity of space, the variety of your creation. We rejoice that you made man to be creative.

The gilded bronze roof of the Pantheon was plundered by Byzantine Emperor Constans II in 655 and replaced with lead in the eighth century.

Colosseum

"It is you, O king, who have grown and become strong; for your greatness has grown and reaches to the heavens, and your dominion to the end of the earth."
Daniel 4:22

Built in about eight years, Rome's Colosseum covers six acres and stands more than 150 feet high. First known as the Flavian Ampitheatre, the arena served Rome for more than 300 years. Made of stone and marble, decorated with statues and huge bronze shields, it was in its day an extravagant structure. Even modern construction techniques would be strained to produce on marshy soil a monument that could last 1,900 years.

Built by the successors of Nero to placate Rome's citizens, the Colosseum offered free entertainment. Many people and animals fought in the Colosseum for the amusement of the jaded Romans. Principally among the victims were gladiators—slaves, criminals, prisoners of war, soldiers of fortune. They fought for great riches or an early death.

In 391 Telemachus, a Christian monk, was horrified to see men killing each other for the entertainment of the crowd. He jumped into the arena to separate the two fighters; angry spectators killed the monk. Telmachus' heroic act is said to have influenced Emperor Honorius to abolish the gladiatorial combats. After the Barbarian invasions, there were no funds available to continue public spectacles in Rome's circuses and arenas. Using the Colosseum's stones, people built houses inside and around the arena. Seven churches were built inside the Colosseum to honor martyrs. Pilgrims came from all over the world to pray at these shrines. Cows and other livestock wandered in the Forum and in Rome's arenas. For centuries wealthy Roman families used the Colosseum as a quarry for stones and artistic treasures to build their palaces. Several severe earthquakes caused great damage to the Colosseum's outside walls, floor, and tiers of seats. In the 19th century Pope Pius VIII prohibited any further demolition of its deteriorating structure. In the 20th century, freezing rain and traffic's rumble further damaged the ruins. Every year the Italian government spends large sums of money repairing the damages of weather and air pollution.

Loving Lord, may our work and our play honor you and do no harm to others.

With 80 exits and its circumference a third of a mile, the Colosseum was massive for its day.

The Mamertine Prison

*"For God has not given us a spirit of fear, but of power and of love and of a sound mind.
Therefore do not be ashamed of the testimony of our Lord, nor of me His prisoner, but share
with me in the sufferings for the gospel according to the power of God."*

II Timothy 1:7-8

The Mamertine Prison, named for Mars, is one of the most ancient sites in Rome.
It was hollowed out of the rock on the back of the Capitoline Hill by Ancus Martius. Later,
Servius Tullius had a lower dungeon excavated from the native rock. One prison was
adequate for all of Rome's prisoners: they might starve to death after a week; they might be
decapitated or slain in the prison. The cold, damp, dark hellhole made it easy for infections
to do their deadly work quickly. It was such a horrible dungeon that as early as 449 B.C.
Appius Claudius and Oppius, prominent government leaders, committed suicide in this
underground prison. From the upper dungeon, prisoners were dropped though an opening
in the floor into the lower dungeon. Bodies were removed through a door that opens into the
underground stream that empties into the Tiber River.

Tourists enter the prison under the porch of the Church of St. Joseph of the
Carpenters and walk down stairs to the lower dungeon. It takes several moments for eyes
to adjust to the windowless room. The dungeon is 16 feet high, 30 feet long, and 22 feet
deep. The sound of running water comes from the *Cloaca Maxima*, or the biggest sewer, an
underground stream that flows constantly, ensuring constant dampness. Gruesome stories
are recorded about the dungeon's victims.

The Mamertine Prison is the accepted place of the imprisonment of Peter and Paul,
possibly during the persecution of A.D. 64. In the lower prison a column is labeled that
Peter and Paul were both chained to it. Legend says they were imprisoned for nine months,
guarded constantly by Roman guards. When the guards, Processus and Martinianus,
made professions of faith in Christ, Peter prayed for water with which to baptize them.
Miraculously, a stream of water sprang out of the ground, and he baptized the guards.

*Father of all mercies, we thank you that whatever life brings our way, your Holy
Spirit is with us to comfort and guide. We thank you for your love and care.*

**Tourists will notice a mark on the wall of the lower dungeon—
kissed by visiting Christians worldwide—
against which St. Peter's head is said to have rested.**

Church of St. Peter-in-Chains

"Most assuredly, I say to you, when you were younger, you girded yourself and walked where you wished; but when you are old, you will stretch out your hands, and another will gird you and carry you where you do not wish."
John 21:18

One Sunday in August when my mother was visiting, we went to the Church of St. Peter-in-Chains. We were intent on seeing Michelangelo's *Moses*, which is on display there. Parking and traffic were easy on a summer afternoon. We entered the large church, built originally in 442 by Empress Eudoxia. Fortunately for us, we were present on August 1, the only day in the year in which the reliquary containing St. Peter's chains is open.

In the Bible, several miracles are attributed to Peter. Even his shadow had miraculous qualities (Acts 5:15). Peter's chains were first mentioned at the Council of Ephesus in 431. Many churches named St. Peter-in-Chains were built in various cities. Often the reliquaries contained filings from the chains in Rome. A placard explained that the chains on display in the church in Rome bound St. Peter during his imprisonment in Jerusalem. Also displayed are chains from a near-by prison, still in use in the fifth century, and are similar to the chains with which Peter was shackled. We waited in line to view and touch the chains in the glass and gold framed box in which they are permanently displayed. The cold, clammy, rusting iron chains were a contrast to the usual relics of martyrs' blood and bones or personal items. The chains had belonged to the Roman government, not an individual.

Tradition says Peter was arrested by Emperor Nero's soldiers, chained, and thrown with the Apostle Paul into prison where the apostles stayed until they were executed. When chained, Peter probably remembered the prophetic words of Christ that he would be bound and taken where he did not want to go. As we touched the chains that memorable day, we were reminded of the price many Christians still pay to live their faith.

Dear Lord, help us to hear your call to service and be obedient to your leading. Help us to be aware that you are always with us.

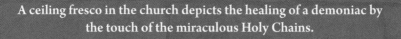

A ceiling fresco in the church depicts the healing of a demoniac by the touch of the miraculous Holy Chains.

St. Peter's Basilica

*"O LORD our God, even this material we have gathered to build a Temple
to honor your holy name comes from you! It all belongs to you!"*
I Chronicles 29:16 (NLT)

According to tradition, in A.D. 67, the Apostle Peter was crucified upside down in the Circus of Nero and Caligula, where thousands of first-century Christians suffered martyrdom. Peter was buried on Vatican Hill in the cemetery near the circus. In A.D. 90 Bishop Anacletus had a small chapel built over his grave. Emperor Constantine, at the request of Pope Sylvester I, destroyed the Circus of Nero and built the first basilica of St. Peter, around 330.

In the 15th century, Pope Nicolas V ordered work on a new building to honor St. Peter. It is this structure that still evokes awe from those who enter its great portals. As Lorenzo, a Vatican guide we knew, said, one could go to St. Peter's every day and see something different with every visit.

The building's beauty and size are overwhelming, but even though it is built on such a grand scale, everything is in balance. Cherubs holding holy water fonts seem small as you enter, but up close, they are more than 6 feet tall. In the floor are the dimensions of the world's greatest cathedrals with St. Peter's the longest church. Of the many artistic treasures present, most famous is Michelangelo's *Pietà*, the marble statue of the Madonna holding the crucified Christ. For centuries the public was allowed to touch the statue, feel the smooth marble. But it is now visible only from behind glass after a crazed fanatic damaged the statue with a hammer in 1972.

The marvelous basilica stands over the church built by Constantine. Some of that basilica may be visited by walking down a stairway near the high altar. Many papal tombs are in the lower level, often referred to as the "grottoes" or "the tomb of the popes." Below the lower basilica are remains of Vatican Hill's ancient Roman cemetery, which may be seen with special permission. Pagan and Christian tombs are conserved, including that of St. Peter.

*Father, Thank you for Simon Peter, and all faithful followers of yours.
May our lives reflect the love of Christ.*

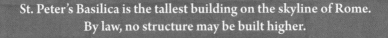

St. Peter's Basilica is the tallest building on the skyline of Rome.
By law, no structure may be built higher.

Obelisk in St. Peter's Square

"Behold, this stone shall be a witness to us."
Joshua 24:27b

The oldest item in St. Peter's Square is the red granite obelisk, brought from the Temple in Heliopolis in Egypt by Emperor Caligula in A.D. 37. For 1,200 years it stood by Constantine's Basilica of St. Peter. Aesthetically, the obelisk didn't belong there, but—weighing one million pounds—it was too large and heavy to move around. Pope Sixtus V asked for suggestions on how to move this heavy treasure. Domenico Fontana presented the pope with a small model crane of wood and an obelisk of lead. The pope ordered Fontana to proceed at once with plans to move the obelisk to St. Peter's Square.

On April 30, 1586, after months of preparation, thousands of Romans came to watch the moving of the obelisk, which was packed in straw mats, encased in wooden planks, and lashed by strong iron bands. At dawn of that historic day, Fontana led 800 laborers to a mass in front of St. Peter's. Standing ready were 140 carthorses. The workers confessed their sins, received communion, and began their tasks. The huge wooden machine that was to lift the obelisk with stout ropes was set in motion by 35 windlasses, each worked by two horses and 10 men. After 12 turns, the obelisk had been raised a foot off its base. People rejoiced, church bells rang, canons fired. The obelisk was hoisted, but not moved.

Erection of the obelisk was set for September 14, the Feast of the Exaltation of the Cross. The pope declared if anyone spoke on this solemn occasion, he would be executed. To raise the obelisk, 140 horses turned 40 windlasses. Working the ropes was a Ligurian sailor who saw that the ropes, heated by friction, were about to burn. Risking his life, he shouted, "Water on the ropes!" People ran for buckets of water to splash on the hot ropes. The ropes cooled and the obelisk was lowered on to the backs of four couchant bronze lions. The brave sailor was rewarded.

Lord, thank you for creative minds and brave hearts that bless us all.

The obelisk is 80 feet high and one piece of granite.

Vatican City

"Behold, bless the LORD, All you servants of the LORD, Who by night stand in the house of the LORD! Lift up your hands in the sanctuary, And bless the LORD."
Psalm 134:1-2

Vatican City is an independent state of 109 acres within the city limits of Rome. Its ruler is the pope. The Vatican sends and receives ambassadors to and from other nations. In ancient Rome, Vatican Hill was the site of a cemetery. Next to the cemetery in imperial times was the Circus of Caligula and Nero, in which the apostle Peter and many early Christians died for their faith. According to legend, Peter was buried in a cemetery on Vatican Hill, the future site of St. Peter's Basilica.

Until 1309, the pope lived in the Lateran Palace, which was deeded to the church by Constantine. In 1377 when the pope returned to Rome from Avignon, France, he moved into the Vatican Palace because the Lateran Palace had been badly burned. Popes took advantage of the skills of numerous artists and architects to embellish and enlarge the church, palace, and administrative buildings. During the Renaissance, many antique statues, carvings, and other treasures were dug up during the building of private palaces and public buildings. These treasures, claimed by the papacy, are in the Vatican Museum, the first museum in Europe.

"The Vatican" is a short name for the official name, "The State of Vatican City." Within the Vatican walls are the papal palace, the Vatican Museum's painting and sculpture galleries, the Vatican Library with a treasure trove of ancient manuscripts and books from all over the world, and the Sistine Chapel. St. Peter's Basilica is the only Vatican building that can be entered freely from the streets of Rome. For entrance to the Vatican Museum, a ticket must be purchased. For entrance into other parts of the Vatican, permission must be secured and an appointment must be made. Vatican Radio has its own headquarters and broadcasts daily all over the world.

Father, thank you for your constant love and care of your children everywhere.

Almost 800 people live within the Vatican's walls.

Sistine Chapel

"Oh come, let us worship and bow down; Let us kneel before the LORD our Maker."
Psalm 95:6

Most people enter the Sistine Chapel with a sense of holy awe. It is one place they want to see. Some rush in, fulfilling a tourist's duty. After walking the long corridors of the Vatican Museum, weary people enter the chapel. They see benches placed around the chapel and rush for the nearest available place. Some young people, oblivious of the religious nature of the chapel, stretch out on the floor and gaze at the ceiling, the most famous painting in the world. No photography is allowed, and no lying on the floor. During the holy year, visitors were asked to stay no more than 10 minutes because of the crowds.

"Sistine" is a derivation of the name "Sixtus." Pope Sixtus IV had Giovanni de Dolci erect the chapel. Florentine masters began decorating the side walls in 1482. Botticelli, Perugina, Rosselli, Pintoricchio, and Ghirlandaio painted colorful scenes from the Bible. In the 16th century Pope Julius II asked Michelangelo to paint the ceiling. The monumental job consumed four years of the life of an artist who considered himself a sculptor. Twenty years later Michelangelo was called again by Pope Paul III to paint the *Last Judgment* on the altar wall of the Sistine Chapel. This gigantic depiction of the end of the age, the separation of good souls from evil ones, took four years of intense effort.

The Sistine Chapel is a place where the pope prays and where he has special services. The College of Cardinals meets in the chapel to elect a new pope when there is a vacancy. In 1978 when Pope Paul VI prayed with the Anglican Archbishop of Canterbury for the first time in the history of the church, representatives of different denominations were also present. My husband was fortunate to be invited to participate in that historic, ecumenical service.

Creative God, thank you for making us as we are.
Help us to enjoy the beauty of your holiness

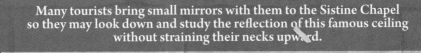

Many tourists bring small mirrors with them to the Sistine Chapel so they may look down and study the reflection of this famous ceiling without straining their necks upward.

Monastery of the Three Fountains

"Be faithful until death, and I will give you the crown of life."
Revelation 2:10b

Il Monasterio delle Tre Fontane, the Monastery of the Three Fountains, occupies the space where the Roman Empire once executed citizens. Citizens were beheaded—not crucified—or thrown to wild animals in the arena. During the Middle Ages, the church acquired the land to preserve this hallowed place.

At the top of the hill is the site of the Apostle Paul's martyrdom and the Church of St. Paul at the Three Fountains. The New Testament gives no details of his death, but strong traditions and public records say what happened here.

The church is carefully tended. Built in the fifth century, it was rebuilt in 1599. In the middle of the floor is a classical design of the four seasons, a mosaic from the ruins of Ostia Antica, ancient port of Rome. In the corner of the dark church is a broken marble column, reputed to be the column on which Paul put his head for the executioner's sword. Legend says the head bounced on the ground, and a healing spring flowed from the ground. The head rolled down the hill, stopped, and another spring flowed, and then the head rolled to a lower level, and a third spring came from the ground. Tradition says one of the springs is cold, one tepid, one hot. Over each spring an altar was built. For centuries pilgrims came to drink the water and be healed by the miraculous springs. Now the fountains are capped.

The monks make and sell extract of eucalyptus for bronchial infections, aromatic vinegar for colds and headaches, and eucalyptus liqueur. They also sell honey from their beehives and arguably the best chocolate in Rome. The visitor can purchase the monks' specialties, but the most important thing one can take away is a profound sense of spiritual peace.

Eternal God, thank you for the courage of Paul and of all others who were faithful unto death.

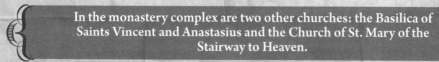

In the monastery complex are two other churches: the Basilica of Saints Vincent and Anastasius and the Church of St. Mary of the Stairway to Heaven.

St. John in Porta Latina and St. John in Oil

"Rest in the LORD, and wait patiently for Him; Do not fret because of him who prospers in his way, Because of the man who brings wicked schemes to pass."
Psalm 37:7

One summer day I drove with a friend across town. Within 15 minutes we arrived at Piazza Numa Pompilio where the Appian Way begins. We had ventured out early to experience the quiet beauty of the Church of St. John in the Latin Gate. The church was built in the fifth century by Gelsius, rebuilt in 772, and reconsecrated in 1191.

We walked to a simple brick church set back in a courtyard. The antiquity of the place gripped us. A tall cedar of Lebanon spreads its branches over the area and shades an ancient white marble well, delicately carved. A superb 12th century bell tower soars above the church. As we entered the arched porch, I noticed that each of the four supporting columns was different from the others. The main apse was pierced by three windows with panes of golden alabaster that allowed light to enter the church. In the chancel's upper windows, thin sheets of selenite filtered light into the clerestory, illuminating damaged frescoes whose surface is flaking off because of centuries of damp and neglect. Antique columns of varying styles lined the aisles. Quiet enveloped us. We sat in deep silence in a place where Christians have worshipped for 1,600 years.

After our prayer time, we walked across the street to a large, woodsy public park that was once the garden of the Scipio family. Nearby is the small chapel of St. John in Oil. Designed by Bramante and restored by Borromini, legend says that Emperor Domitian ordered St. John to be thrown into a vat of boiling oil near the Latin Gate. The attempt to kill him was not successful. "He came forth as from a refreshing bath," an event that is said to have occurred before John was exiled to Patmos, where he lived until his death.

God of All Comfort, keep us in perfect peace when difficulties confront us. Help us focus our thoughts on you.

The miracle of St. John surviving Emperor Domitian's oil is celebrated every May 6.

Tomb of Hadrian

"For He shall give His angels charge over you, To keep you in all your ways."
Psalm 91:11

The Tomb of Augustus in Mars Field was full of royals when Hadrian ordered a new tomb to be built for himself and his successors. The Tomb of Hadrian was built of brick and stone and covered with white marble. On top was a mound of earth, planted with a cypress grove, as in the Etruscan manner. Emperors from Hadrian, who died in 138, to Caracalla, who died in 217, were buried there.

In 537 the tomb was used as a garrison. From then on, this tomb was used as a fortress and was the military stronghold of Rome for 1,000 years. On the roof is a bronze statue of an angel sheathing his sword. In 590 a plague was decimating the population of Rome. Pope Gregory the Great led a procession to St. Peter's Basilica to pray for the city. While he was crossing the bridge to go to the basilica, he saw on the mausoleum's summit an angel sheathing a bloody sword, while a choir of angels sang. The bronze statue commemorates this vision and the cessation of the plague. An elevated brick corridor was constructed from the Vatican to the castle in 1277. In times of siege, the pope took refuge in this pile of stone that could accommodate hundreds of soldiers and Vatican officials.

Tourists enter the castle, now a museum, by means of a drawbridge and walk over the moat that made it difficult for Rome's enemies to gain entrance. There are small replicas of the castle at many stages through its history. An amazing collection of ancient weapons is displayed. There are storerooms, the former Vatican treasury, and lavish papal apartments.

When exiting, tourists see the beautiful Bridge of the Angels with statues designed by Bernini. From this bridge, Pope Gregory had seen the Angel Gabriel. Each of Bernini's angels holds a symbol of the passion of Christ.

We are grateful, Lord, that you protect and keep us every day.

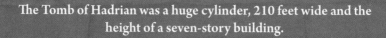

The Tomb of Hadrian was a huge cylinder, 210 feet wide and the height of a seven-story building.

Piazza Navona

"Fear God and give glory to Him, for the hour of His judgment has come; and worship Him who made heaven and earth, the sea and springs of water."
Revelation 14:7

Piazza Navona has always been a place for fun and games. Emperor Domitian built a stadium on the spot almost 2,000 years ago. He called it Circus Agonalis. Here people engaged in athletic displays; they did not fight to the death, as in the Colosseum. Until as late as 1450 the structure of the circus was still very much as it was during the Empire. In the Middle Ages jousts and games of horseshoes were enjoyed by spectators who sat on the original marble seats.

In the early 19th century a summer water festival featured decorated carriages that were driven around the flooded square. By then, apartment buildings, the Pamphili Palace, and two churches had been built on the ruins of the elongated horseshoe stadium. Picturesque, baroque, and overdone, the piazza is embellished by three fountains designed by Bernini. The central fountain, the Fountain of the Four Rivers, is topped by an obelisk, known as Domitian's obelisk, which had stood in the center of the Circus of Maxentius on the Appian Way. The figures around the fountain represent what the sculptor thought were the largest rivers of the world—the Danube, Nile, Platt, and Indus rivers.

Something interesting is always happening in Piazza Navona. Artists display and sell their paintings. Hungry sidewalk artists hurriedly sketch a caricature in a few minutes or a color portrait in half an hour. Strolling vendors sell souvenirs, toys, costume jewelry, clothing. A strolling violinist plays Italian dances. An old man, hungry, walks from table to table at sidewalk restaurants, strums a few chords on an old polished mandolin, and extends his hand for a donation. Romans meet their friends at Piazza Navona. Young people ride around on motor bikes. Tourists stare at tourists and native Romans, and all enjoy the occasion of being together.

Father, thank you for places where people can come together
and enjoy friends, good food, and beauty.

The square's name was corrupted in time to *n'Agona*, to become eventually Piazza Navona.

Basilica of St. John in Lateran

"Praise the LORD! Praise God in His sanctuary; Praise Him in His mighty firmament!"
Psalm 150:1

When Constantine defeated Maxentius at the Battle of the Milvian Bridge, he rode into Rome bearing the sign of the cross. Constantine determined that he would make a gift to God. He owned property of the Lateran family through his second wife and gave this land for a church: the Basilica of St. John in Lateran. It is said that Constantine himself worked on its erection. This cathedral in Rome has been honored as the church of which the pope is the pastor. At the Lateran Council of 1215, the doctrine of the Trinity was clarified, a church inquisition was approved, and it was decided that every Catholic must go to confession and receive the Eucharist at least once a year.

The building that now stands in a very busy neighborhood of the city has changed much from the time when the area looked more like the country than the city. In the fifth century, it was almost destroyed by the Vandals, but restored by Pope Leo the Great. An earthquake in 896 did extensive damage. Its wooden roof and other combustible components were burned in a fire in 1308. It was rebuilt, but burned again in 1360. In 1646 Borromini directed a restoration. Architect Alessandro Galilei devised a classical effect with columns. On the roof are gigantic statues, representing Christ, John the Baptist, John the beloved disciple, and 12 doctors of the church. The main bronze door is from the Senate House in the Forum.

Inside the church, large statues of the 12 apostles, designed by Bernini, line the nave. There are paintings of popes and martyrs, Bible stories in bas relief, and tombs of popes and nobles. The ceiling was designed by Giacomo della Porta. Over the altar two reliquaries are said to contain the heads of Peter and Paul and the table on which Peter served the Lord's Supper.

We worship you in our hearts, O Lord, and praise you in our daily lives

On November 9, 324, St. John in Lateran,
the first Christian basilica, was dedicated.

Villa Borghese Park

*"The LORD God planted a garden eastward in Eden,
and there He put the man whom He had formed."*
Genesis 2:8

Rome's Central Park attracts people like a magnet draws iron. The Villa Borghese Park is big, beautiful, and free to all, a priceless respite for Romans in their busy, raucous city. In every season, it is a joy to stroll on any lane in the various sections of the vast park. It was primarily the creation of Cardinal Scipione Borghese, nephew of Pope Paul V, who began to buy the land shortly after his uncle was elected pope in the early 17th century. By 1650 the circumference of the walls was four kilometers. Inspired by Hadrian's Villa at Tivoli, the park was a playground for the wealthy Borghese family and their aristocratic friends.

The Pincian Gardens, often called the *Pincio*, are located on the north corner of the gardens. At Piazzale Napoleone I is an overlook of Rome with one of the best views of the city. At the opposite corner of the large park is the Casino of the Villa Borghese, often referred to as the Borghese Gallery. Cardinal Borghese had the palace built for the purpose of entertaining friends and displaying his art collection. Receptions and gatherings of titled families were held in the palace and in adjoining patios and gardens. Ancient Roman and Greek statues, mosaics, and splendid marble sculptures by Canova and Bernini delight the eye. Paintings by Raphael, Titian, Caravaggio, and other great Italian painters decorate the walls.

A 19th-century travel book warns against going to the Borghese Park in summer because one would contract malaria: "If you come hither in summer, and stray through these glades in the golden sunset, fever walks arm-in-arm with you, and death awaits you in the end of the dim vista." Fortunately for 21st-century strollers, one no longer risks feverish death by strolling on a warm summer day in Rome's delightful Borghese gardens.

Creator of beauty, thank you for gardens that enhance our lives.

**Two hundred paintings from the Borghese Gallery were sold to
Napoleon and are in the Louvre in Paris.**

Protestant Cemetery

"Then the righteous will shine forth as the sun in the kingdom of their Father."
Matthew 13:43a

The Pyramid of Caius Cestius was built about 30 B.C. as a mausoleum for a Roman prefect who had traveled in Egypt and been impressed by the pyramids at Giza. The Apostle Paul walked past it on his way to be executed during Nero's reign. Almost 300 years ago an area next to the pyramid was set aside as a place for the burial of non-Catholics.

Widely known as the Protestant Cemetery—although it contains the graves of Jews and other non-Christians—it is officially named *Cimitero Acattolic,* the "non-Catholic cemetery." It is also referred to as *Cimitero degli Inglesi,* the "English cemetery."

In his preface to *Adonais*—an elegy for his friend John Keats—Percy Shelley wrote, "The cemetery is an open space among the ruins, covered in winter with violets and daisies. It might make one in love with death to think that one should be buried in so sweet a place." Keats is buried there. If a caretaker is on duty, tourists may walk to Keats' tomb, located to the far left, as one enters the iron gates. But even when the cemetery is locked, tourists can look through a hole in the wall and read his tombstone.

There are other tombs to see, the pyramid, and the numerous cats that live around it. Many people walk to Shelley's tomb, whose body was washed up on the beach at Lerici, near Livorno. Shelley's body was burned on the beach, and his heart was brought to Rome to his widow, Mary Shelley. The painter John Severn, a friend of Keats', and author Edward John Trelawney, a friend of Shelley's, are also buried there.

We are grateful, dear Lord, that you are with us wherever we go.

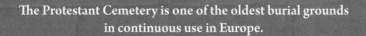

The Protestant Cemetery is one of the oldest burial grounds in continuous use in Europe.

Victor Emmanuel Monument

"My son, fear the LORD and the king."
Proverbs 24:21a

British soldiers nicknamed the colossal monument to King Victor Emmanuel II, "The Wedding Cake." Italians refer to it as the "Olivetti typewriter" or the "inkpot." Begun in 1885, it took 26 years to build. The monument honors the united Italy and marks a new beginning for an ancient people. The architect, G. Sacconi, designed a monument that would reflect the glory of the Roman Empire, cover the northern hillside of the Capitoline Hill, and would be seen from the Vatican. He planned it to be tall enough for the pope to see every morning when he went to his window to look over the city his predecessors had ruled. The equestrian statue of the king is in gilded bronze. The statue is huge; the moustache of the king is a meter long. The base on which the equestrian statue stands is called the "Altar of the Fatherland." In it is buried Italy's "unknown soldier" who fought in World War I. Heads of state come to the monument to lay wreaths on the soldier's tomb.

Discriminating Italians object to the choice of stone of which the monument is made—white Brescian marble—instead of Roman travertine, which gives most of the city a honey glow. Some people think it is too large and completely out of character with Piazza Venezia. Italians have talked of destroying the monument, but a 1983 survey among public figures was almost unanimous in stating that the monument should be left standing. Its large space is a popular place for public demonstrations and gatherings. During World War II, newsreels showed Benito Mussolini haranguing huge crowds to fight for the glory of the fatherland from the upper portico.

One Sunday afternoon, soon after our arrival in Italy, our family of three climbed the steps of the Victor Emmanuel Monument. A spectacular view of Rome was our reward.

God of grace and God of glory, on your people pour your power.

Possibly the largest monument in the world, the Victor Emmanuel Monument is more than 500 feet long and 250 feet high.

Trastevere

"Then Miriam the prophetess, the sister of Aaron, took the timbrel in her hand; and all the women went out after her with timbrels and with dances."
Exodus 15:20

Rome's residents who live across the Tiber from the eastern, main part of the city inhabit the area known as Trastevere. They think of themselves as the original Romans. The ancient community welcomed travelers who came by river to live and work in Rome. Because of a hybrid population, this part of Rome, separated by the river, was a distinct entity. The Trastevere dialect was very different than Rome's. Two piazzas and two streets honor her famous poets who wrote in dialect.

The churches of Trastevere are many and ancient. One of the most beautiful is Santa Maria in Trastevere. Founded by St. Calixtus in 224, it is alleged to be the first church in Rome dedicated to the Virgin Mary. There is a legend that a fountain of pure oil sprang up on the spot at the time of the birth of Jesus. It gushed for one day and flowed into the Tiber. In early times, the church was called *Fons Olei* for the "Oil Fountain." Through the centuries, the church was built and rebuilt, always grander than before. It is now embellished with works of art and with colorful mosaics on the façade and inside.

Palazzo Corsini and Villa Farnesina are two of the most interesting spots in Trastevere. Raphael and his school painted many frescoes in rooms and halls in the Farnesina. The palace was built for Agostino Chigi, a great art patron, who entertained lavishly. After his elaborate banquets, the servants threw the gold and silver plates into the Tiber as a final show of extravagance. Unknown to the guests, huge fishing nets had been let down into the river. The valuables were retrieved the next day.

Trastevere celebrates itself in July. *Noiantri* combines ancient and modern festivities. Streets are decorated with lights. Fireworks, dancing in the piazzas, open air movies, concerts, and serenades on the streets are enjoyed.

Father, thank you for communities that value the past and build for the future.

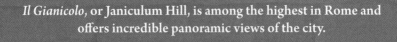

Il Gianicolo, or Janiculum Hill, is among the highest in Rome and offers incredible panoramic views of the city.

Villa d'Este

"I will give of the fountain of the water of life freely to him who thirsts."
Revelation 21:6b

Sparkling fountains, moss-draped grottoes, ponds filled with water lilies, paths edged with ilexes, and a hilltop villa with a view await the persistent tourist. Located about 15 miles northeast of Rome on Via Tiburtina, Villa d'Este is in the town of Tivoli. When its founder, Cardinal Ippolito d'Este, entered Tivoli to take up his post of governor, he began to plan the construction of a magnificent summer residence. He appropriated part of the Franciscan convent attached to the Church of Santa Maria Maggiore, high on a hill in the town center. He ordered the demolition of 40 houses to provide adequate space for his house and gardens within the city walls. Building began in 1560.

The architect, Pirro Ligorio, an expert on classical sculpture, was directing excavations in Hadrian's Villa several miles away. As ancient marbles and statues were uncovered at Hadrian's Villa, many of these were brought to Villa d'Este. The Cardinal established in his villa some learned academies, discussions on theology and philosophy, theatrical performances, and concerts. The Tiber River was diverted through the gardens. Many fountains were created of stone with stucco relief. Their water sprays, shoots upwards, runs downhill in little waterfalls, collects in ponds, and eventually flows back into the river. Walking by the Hundred Fountains on a hot summer day is sheer pleasure. The Fountain of the Dragons is dramatic, whether viewed from the villa or from below. Originally, the Fountain of the Dragons had contraptions that made the water sound like cannon shot. The Organ Fountain no longer plays melodies, but offers an impressive view from the upper level. The Owl Fountain emitted sounds of singing birds and a screeching owl. Today only the sounds of flowing water are heard. Serving as the background for a small open-air theater is the Rometta Fountain, a miniature construction of ancient Rome.

God of all beauty and wonder, help us, your children,
to use wisely the earth's resources.

Completed in 1572, Villa d'Este is now owned by the Italian Government and is open to the public.

Castelli Romani

"I will say of the LORD, 'He is my refuge and my fortress; My God, in Him I will trust.'"
Psalm 91:2

From ancient times Romans have been attracted to an area southeast of the city in the Alban Hills known as the *Castelli Romani*, or "Roman Castles." The area spreads for several miles into the countryside. The airy climate and distant views of the sea attract Italians as a pleasant area in which to live or to have a second home for weekends and summers. A dozen interesting communities make up the Castelli Romani, but two of them are special.

Castel Gandolfo is a town located off the New Appian Way. It is on a hill overlooking Lago Albano. The pope's summer palace, also known as Castel Gandolfo, is at the end of the main street. Not open to visitors, the faithful gather in front of the castle's main gates for papal blessings on Wednesdays when he is in residence, usually from late June until mid-September. The pope stands on a second floor balcony and can be seen from the main entrance. Baroque castle was erected in 1628 by Maderno, who also designed the façade of St. Peter's. It is built on the ruins of Domitian's villa.

Frascati has long been a favorite of Rome's fashionable, wealthy people. The town's fame is based on its patrician villas and its white wine. Sixteenth- and 17th-century villas are set in terraced gardens, among ancient oaks and twisted plane trees. There are grottoes, statues, and fountains to enhance the beauty of these ostentatious houses and grounds. During the Empire, Cicero lived in the Tuscolo mansion, built on the hill overlooking Frascati. Tour groups and ordinary Roman residents enjoy a drive to Frascati for excellent food, fresh air, and marvelous views. The name Frascati began as an insignificant village where the roofs of its houses were covered with *frasche*, or "small boughs." Insignificant no more, Frascati to a modern Italian means good wine, good living.

*Loving Father, Thank you for the calmness that fills our souls
when we live in harmony with you and with our fellowman.*

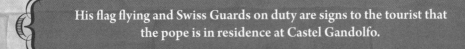

His flag flying and Swiss Guards on duty are signs to the tourist that
the pope is in residence at Castel Gandolfo.

Villa of Tiberius

"After these things Jesus went over the Sea of Galilee, which is the Sea of Tiberias. Then a great multitude followed Him, because they saw His signs which He performed on those who were diseased."
John 6:1-2

Perched high on a bluff on the island of Capri, the ruins of the Villa of Tiberius are a major tourist sight. The extensive ruins command beautiful views from this romantic spot off Italy's western coast. Emperor Tiberius ruled the Roman Empire during the life of Jesus Christ. Heir and successor of Augustus, Tiberius did not want to be emperor. He detested his duties.

Tiberius spent as much time as possible at his beautiful Capri retreat where he cavorted with beautiful young women. Messages were signaled from Capri to the mainland by torch, then relayed all the way to Rome. When the emperor was away from Rome, there were no public shows and festivals. Without its games, Rome was a dull place, and the people resented his absence.

In the ruins, a tourist guide relates this story: Tiberius felt secure that his palace on Capri was inaccessible to his enemies. One day a fisherman appeared on the grounds. He had caught some fish and, thinking the emperor would enjoy them, he climbed the bluff, using a secret way he had known since childhood. Surprised, Tiberius asked the fisherman about his secret path up the cliff. When convinced that only the fisherman knew how to climb the precipice, the emperor thanked the fisherman for his kindness. Tiberius had his guards escort the fisherman to the edge of the cliff and throw him into the sea.

On his way to Rome for a visit, he stopped when he saw a bad omen: a snake being eaten by a swarm of ants. He interpreted this as a warning that the Roman mob would destroy him if he entered the city. The emperor turned back toward Capri, but he died before leaving the mainland. Romans rejoiced at the death of the strange emperor who preferred solitude to shows.

Father, help us accept life's responsibilities with mature faith, knowing that you always strengthen us to accomplish the tasks to which you call us.

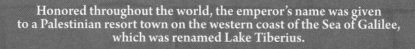
Honored throughout the world, the emperor's name was given to a Palestinian resort town on the western coast of the Sea of Galilee, which was renamed Lake Tiberius.

from Cholera to Capri

"To everything there is a season, A time for every purpose under heaven: …
A time to kill, And a time to heal."
Ecclesiastes 3:1, 3a

Axel Munthe, a Swedish intellectual, completed medical studies in 1881 and planned for a holiday before beginning his medical practice. Before setting out on his adventure, he read a newspaper account of a cholera epidemic in Naples. The idealistic young doctor purchased all the medicines he could afford, bought a train ticket to Naples, and left immediately to help. For two years he helped those he could. One of his colleagues, a Red Cross worker, was impressed with the way the young doctor unselfishly helped others. When the epidemic was over, she urged Munthe to start a medical practice in Rome.

Munthe established a very successful practice. He enjoyed Rome and lived in an apartment at Piazza di Spagna where John Keats had died. One night, hearing knocking, Munthe opened the door and saw a frightened woman who asked if there was some place she could look out on the Spanish Steps. Through the window they saw a man. When he disappeared from sight, she said that she was safe. "Wasn't that Gabriel d'Annunzio?" asked Munthe. "Yes, and I am Eleonora Duse," said the greatest actress of her time. The famous playwright had written many plays for her. They were at a party when they began to quarrel, and he threatened to kill her. She had fled to the nearest place she could find. This incident was described in a letter from Italy's ambassador to England to Munthe's son and is on display at the Keats-Shelley Museum.

Munthe's medical career was spent in Rome and his retirement years on Capri. In the late 19th century, many archeological discoveries were being made there. Munthe acquired many treasures for his charming hilltop villa and gardens he named for St. Michael. The house is furnished with 17th-century furniture. There is a steady stream of tourists to this home, now a museum. From vine-covered walks, they enjoy magnificent vistas of the blue Mediterranean.

Compassionate Father, help us to learn compassion for those in distress.

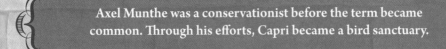

Axel Munthe was a conservationist before the term became common. Through his efforts, Capri became a bird sanctuary.

Sardinia

"Their fish will be of the same kinds as the fish of the Great Sea, exceedingly many."
Ezekiel 47:10b

Named for a tiny fish, Italians call the island of Sardinia, *Sardegna*. One hundred miles from the Italian peninsula, this sun-blessed destination is reached from mainland Europe by ferries, ships, and more than 100 airline connections each day. Compared to Italians on the mainland, Sardinians lead simple lives as shepherds, mountaineers, and fishermen. For centuries malaria, poverty, and banditry made life difficult for the Sards and kept visitors away.

From ancient times, Cretans, Phoenicians, Greeks, Romans, Vandals, Byzantines, Pisans, and Genoese colonized the island. In recent centuries, Spanish, Austrians, and Italians laid claim to this rocky island. Sardinia played a vital part in the unification of Italy in the 19th century and is now an autonomous region with a large measure of administrative freedom.

Today's zinc and lead mines, petrochemical and chemical industries, salt works, an aluminum plant, and a growing tourist industry help bring this island province into the 21st century. The sandy, sunny beaches lure northern Europeans and Italians in summer months. When not sunning on the beaches of the Costa Smeralda, tourists enjoy exploring the prehistoric fortress houses. These conical structures were built with huge blocks of stone, laid one on top of another without mortar. Bronze statues found in these ancient structures and in tombs are on display in a museum in Cagliari, the capitol of Sardinia.

When flying over the island, one sees heavy concentration of residence on coastal areas and few homes or settlements in the central part of the island. Ninety percent of the island is mountainous. One of the challenges to this rapidly changing area is the preservation of its ancient traditions, beautiful landscape, fine beaches, and clear waters. Traditional handcrafts include basket weaving, ceramics, coral, and the weaving of carpets, tapestries, and fabrics. Like all islanders, Sardinians are hospitable, serving homemade wines, goat cheese, ham, or fish.

Thank you, Father, for the wonder of the beautiful seas
and for nature's abundance.

Sardinia is the second largest Mediterranean island, measuring more than 9,300 square miles.

Naples

*"God is our refuge and strength, A very present help in trouble.
Therefore we will not fear, Even though the earth be removed, And
though the mountains be carried into the midst of the sea."*
Psalm 46:1-2

Naples is the third largest city of Italy, the most crowded in Europe. Named Parthenope, it was founded about 750 B.C. by the Greeks, about the time the Latins founded Rome. Later the name was changed to Neapolis and then to *Napoli*, as the Italians know it. Behind the city is the Vomero Hill and in front is the beautiful blue Tyrrhenian Sea. With no space for parks or broad avenues, land is at a premium. Living quarters are crowded, but the sun is ever-shining, the sea air is bracing, and views of Capri and Mt. Vesuvius are life-enhancing.

Street-smart Neapolitans learn early to protect themselves from thieves and robbers and to look after themselves. Having lived with the constant threat of the eruption of a volcano, a natural disaster from the sea, invading armies, or crushing poverty, the indomitable Neapolitans sing and eat their way through life as if they have no care in the world. They are hard workers. Poverty has forced them to be creative in order to live. A few of the results of their creativity are good, inexpensive food; emotional love songs that touch the heart; and a courageous, triumphant acceptance of life and its challenges. Pizza is native to Naples as are pasta and mozzarella cheese. It was said in Naples that, "Fishermen eat like kings, and the King eats like fishermen."

The *Camorra*, the Neapolitan version of the Mafia, had its grip on Naples until a group of concerned citizens decided to reclaim their city. In 1980 Baroness Mirella Barrocca organized the rich and powerful of the city into the Committee Naples Ninety-Nine. A new, honest and determined mayor in the 1990s cooperated with law enforcement and city planners to control traffic and illegal parking, eliminate crime, and repair churches and museums. Now tourists feel safer to walk its streets and enjoy the city.

*Thank you, Lord, for the beauties of nature and the creativity of mankind.
Help us enjoy our lives.*

**Naples' Archeological Museum houses the treasures of
Pompeii and Herculaneum.**

Pompeii

*"Then you shall flee through My mountain valley,
For the mountain valley shall reach to Azal. Yes, you shall flee As you fled from the
earthquake In the days of Uzziah king of Judah."*
Zechariah 14:5a

Pompeii, a city on the Tyrrhenian Sea south of Naples, had a lovely view of Vesuvius, thought to be an extinct volcano. The volcanic soil supported an agricultural economy. Grapes, other fruits, and a wide variety of vegetables grew there. Cattle and sheep thrived in that sun-kissed land. Fishing was good. Today it is one of the best-known ancient cities because of the eruption of Vesuvius on August 24, 79. Modern tourists include Pompeii and neighboring Herculaneum in a day's excursion.

Pompeii's walls enclosed an oval-shaped city about two miles in circumference. Eight gates allowed entrance into the city during the day. Inhabitants built their villas in the typical Roman style with rooms grouped around an open atrium or reception room. A pool in the center of the atrium caught rainwater. Wealthy citizens decorated rooms with frescoes and mosaics, often using themes of classical mythology. Red walls were popular in living and dining rooms.

An eye-witness account was written by Pliny the Younger, describing how he led his mother to safety through the deadly fumes, hot ash, and falling stones. His uncle, Pliny the Elder, another Roman writer, escaped from Pompeii but returned with a fleet of ships to rescue some people and observe the phenomenon. Overcome by fumes, the older Pliny died on the shore.

Because of a changed seacoast, it was impossible for survivors to locate the buried city. In 1748 a peasant, digging in his vineyard, discovered a wall, and the excavation of the city began. Archeologists constantly make new discoveries in the ruins. They also repair damage from earthquakes of recent years. In hardened ash, scientists find the shells of bodies of fallen people. By carefully pouring plaster into the shells, scientists make detailed copies of Pompeii's fleeing citizens, many with agonized facial expressions. The National Museum in Naples and the museum at Pompeii display many artifacts.

Father, thank you for modern science that helps us learn from the past.

During its life, Pompeii grew to be a city of 20,000 people.

Amalfi Coast

"Let the heavens rejoice, and let the earth be glad; Let the sea roar, and all its fullness."
Psalm 96:11

Brightly colored fishing boats lie on the beaches or at anchor in the bays along the Amalfi Coast, south of Naples. The rocky peninsula is encircled by a winding, two-lane road. A bus trip from Sorrento to Salerno along this coast provides an opportunity to focus on views of sparkling blue water and to photograph spectacular scenes of sea, beaches, and villages hanging on to steep hillsides. White cubicle houses contrast with green gardens and blue sky and sea. Grape vines and citrus and olive trees are caressed by a constant sea breeze. Huge rocks that long ago tumbled down from the hills rest on some of the beaches. Some beaches are covered with pebbles, and some have sandy coves, reached by steep paths from the highway. Villas, hotels, chapels, and garages are cantilevered over the vertical terrain. Heavy traffic is controlled by seasonal rules.

On November 24, 1343, an earthquake with resulting landslides caused half of the city to drop into the sea. Amalfi never fully recovered, but the tourist should walk through the town. Steep steps lead to the entrance of the Cathedral of San Andrea where, according to tradition, the body of St. Andrew the Apostle is buried. Outside of town a former Cappuchin convent clings to a hillside. Now a hotel, it has comfortable rooms, great food, a cloister, and fantastic views.

Several caves, grottoes, and caverns on the Amalfi Coast are worth exploring. At the mouth of the Emerald Grotto reflections of light pass through the water, producing unusual color effects. Pandona Grotto at Maiori is one of the most picturesque caves. Many tourists remember a drive along the Amalfi Coast as the most beautiful experience of their tour of Italy.

God of land and sea, thank you for the splendor of your creation
and for eyes to see its wonders.

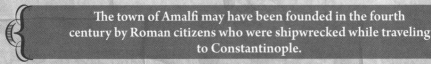

The town of Amalfi may have been founded in the fourth
century by Roman citizens who were shipwrecked while traveling
to Constantinople.

City on the Toe

"After three months we sailed in an Alexandrian ship whose figurehead was the Twin Brothers, which had wintered at the island. And landing at Syracuse, we stayed three days. From there we circled round and reached Rhegium."
Acts 28:11-13a

On the toe of the boot of Italy is Reggio Calabria, the capital of the southern province of Calabria. The name distinguishes it from Reggio Emilia near Bologna. Many trains from the north terminate at Reggio where the traveler may catch a boat to other Mediterranean ports. Someday there may be a bridge from Reggio to Sicily. Reggio Calabria is a long day's drive from Rome. Calabria generally has good weather. There are good ski runs, beaches, and good hunting. Ferries take tourists back and forth from the mainland to Sicily. During summer holidays, automobile waiting lines for ferries are long.

Calabria is steeped in history. One sees Greek and Roman ruins, 13th-century forts and castles, and Byzantine and Norman churches, which often are incorporated into later structures. Many different invaders came to the area and left their marks in architecture, customs, and in the genetic make-up of the people.

Many writers have written about Italy's south. During World War II, when exiled by Mussolini to Eboli in southern Italy, Italian Jewish journalist Carlo Levi wrote the book *Christ Stopped at Eboli*. South of Eboli, the towns are small and poor and few cultural benefits are available for young people. Levi's idea was that the south was so harsh and forbidding that even Christ himself would not go past Eboli. The resultant traditional religion, he insinuated, was a blend of ancient pagan forms, plus what little Christianity could trickle down from the north. The book, made into a realistic film, revealed the plight of southern Italy. An Italian TV documentary on the agricultural and economic problems of Calabria stated that if change is to come in the south, there must be a change in the defeatist philosophy of southern Italians. Religious leaders say a strong, Christian witness is needed to give people hope.

Father, we pray for pastors, isolated priests,
and stalwart Christians who embody your love.

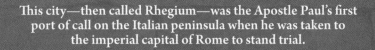

This city—then called Rhegium—was the Apostle Paul's first port of call on the Italian peninsula when he was taken to the imperial capital of Rome to stand trial.

Sicily

"My righteousness is near, My salvation has gone forth, And My arms will judge the peoples; The coastlands will wait upon Me, And on My arm they will trust."
Isaiah 51:5

The largest Mediterranean island, Sicily is roughly triangular in shape. It is separated from mainland Italy by the Strait of Messina. With several small islands, it forms the Italian province of Sicily. It covers almost 10,000 square miles and has a population of about five million people. About 580 B.C. Sicily was part of Magna Grecia, a Grecian empire including southern Italy.

People from every geographical direction have conquered Sicily. Each conqueror left its mark on the island through agriculture, language, religion, customs, and genetics. They were Greeks, Romans, Vandals, Ostrogoths, Byzantines, Saracens, Normans, Germans, French, Spanish, Austrians, Italians under Giuseppe Garibaldi, and American and British troops during World War II. Despite the domination of many foreign rulers, Sicilians maintain pride in their heritage and an amazing ability to endure hardship. Sicilians are bound closely by ties of family and community. Because of years of foreign rule, they distrust government and depend on family and close connections. Today the region of Sicily is one of Italy's 20 governmental units. A 90-member parliament is elected from its nine provinces. Sicily also sends representatives to the Italian parliament in Rome.

Sicily is essentially a plateau but is covered by mountains and hills. The mild climate is good for growing almonds, citrus fruit, olives, grapes, wheat, oregano, and sumac, used in tanning and dyeing. Sicily is one of the principal sources of the world's supply of sulfur. Rock salt and asphalt are also mined. The petrochemical industry is located mostly on the eastern side of the island. The main ports of Palermo, Catania, and Messina send Sicily's products to world markets. Tourists come to see Greek ruins, museums, and cathedrals and to experience the special quality of an island culture. Best seen in spring when almond trees are in bloom, Sicily captivates travelers with its special allure.

We are grateful, our Father, for the world's variety of people, culture, and geography, and we are grateful for goodness everywhere.

Mount Etna, an active volcano, is the island's highest peak at 11,122 feet. Sicily is on a fault in the Mediterranean and suffers frequent earthquakes.

Maps

Temple de la Sibylle à Tivoli.

Rome, le Colysée.

Gravé par Sorgeoller.   Dessiné par Dictionnaire Géographe.   La Lettre par Id.

Revue par Th. Charier.

Imp^te Migeon, Chemin des Plantes, 5, Petit Vanves.

Italy

Lake Magiore
Lake Lugano
Lake Como
Lake Garda
Milan
Verona
Venice
Turin
Cremona
Bologna
Genoa
Ravenna
Monterosso al Mare
Corniglia
Vernazza
Riomaggiore
Manarola
Pisa
Florence
Perugia
Assisi
Elba
Viterbo
Rome
Naples
Pompeii
Amalfi Coast
Capri

Adriatic Sea

Sardinia

Tyrrhenian Sea

Reggio Calabria

Sicily

Mediterranean Sea

Scriptural Index

Scriptural Index

Geographical Index

Geographical Index

Acknowledgements

For the preparation of this manuscript, I would like to thank the many people who encouraged me to write about my experiences and especially those who continued to ask me about the development of the book.

Special thanks to Dr. Joe Baskin for directing me to his former student Lana Neal Shealy, assistant publisher at Xyzzy Press, and to Joe and Ann for reading the manuscript. My skilled editor, Sonua Bohannon, shaped the manuscript into this book, and Jim Stewart, publisher, had the grace, insight, and temerity to publish it.

Special thanks to John and Dorothy Steen for encouraging me to write and share my stories. Also to Peggy Plummer, Pearl DuVall, Dr. Marcie Hinton, Dr. John and Ruthy Countryman, Donna Siebert, Sandi Duranti, Dr. Stanley and Patsy Crabb, Dr. Ross West, Cathy Hodgdon, the Craighead family, Joel and Jean Fletcher, Dr. John Hodges and Susan, and many others who read all or parts of the manuscript and made suggestions.

For Rome, Georgia's, Fahy Store Trip from Rome to Rome, I am ever grateful to Mr. Merle Hardaker (deceased) for their customers' contest with its life-changing impact on the Ruchti ministry. Most of all, I am thankful for God's abundant blessings and guidance.

For my interest in learning and travel, I acknowledge the influence of my parents, family, and teachers. For my acquisition of Italian and understanding of Italian life, I remember Prof. Enzo Amorini, Signorina Viscardi, Anna Maria Ciambella, the Poggi family, Anna Rappocciolo, and colleagues in Italy. The American Women's Association of Rome and Rome Baptist Church (English language) provided opportunities for enjoying and learning about Rome.

Many history, art history, church history, and guidebooks helped me through the years. Outstanding among these are *The Wonders of Rome* by Joseph Fattorusso (The Medici Art Series), *The Companion Guide to Rome* by Georgina Masson (Harper and Row), and *The Italians* by Luigi Barzini (Antheneum Publishers). For practical, accurate travel information, I currently rely on Rick Steves' *Italy* (Avalon Travel).